Foreword by Monica Moss

Radical Love
Your Path to Freedom and Bliss

Melanie Foote-Davis

Ms. Johnson-McClinton
May your life be filled with
joy.
To your Love + freedom,

Editing by Beverly F. Thompson and Z. Elaine Romeo
Illustrations by Nikelle Adams, nikL Designs
Book Design by Nikelle Adams, nikL Designs
Author Photography by Ken Harris Ny-Ke Image Studio
Author Make-Up by Masika Pointer

ISBN-13: 978-1518729010
ISBN-10: 1518729010

Library of Congress Cataloging-in-Publication Data
Foote-Davis, Melanie, 2015

This book is dedicated to my mother, Thelma E. Foote.

Mom, they say a picture speaks more than a thousand words. I experienced the richness of God's love through watching you. I am a witness to your unwavering faith, commitment and dedication to Jesus Christ. You made sure my siblings and I also knew God.

Mom it was evident that you were fully committed to this mission. It is demonstrated through your actions. It's genuine and seeps from your heart through the essence of your being. You are an African-American woman who lived through segregation. Yet I've never seen an inkling of prejudice or hatred in your eyes. We are all God's children and you taught us to treat everyone as someone worthy of love. I have watched you greet total strangers with hugs and that infectious laugh of yours with no regard to race, gender, stature or status.

You have such a strong dedication to serve. I don't recall ever hearing you say that you were too tired to honor your commitments. There is a lot to say about a woman who raised eight children, worked full-time at an elementary school, and maintained your desire to teach songs to and play the piano for the youth choir. For the love of God, you worked well into your seventies at the Youth Center tutoring kids with homework until your health dictated otherwise.

Mom you are my first love. I may not have memories of it, but I know this from the depths of my soul that I learned how to love in your womb. It is because of you that I understand the power of having a voice. When I was a young girl and well into my teens, you allowed me to be heard. You taught me the power of the pen when I didn't have the courage to speak with you face to face. I could write to you about anything. Afterward, we'd sit down and have a rich discussion about it.

Mom, you not only gave me permission to find my voice, you created a safe space for me to grow at my own pace. I had some hard knocks along the way. You distanced yourself enough for me to feel to free, but stayed close enough to reach you when I needed you most.

Mom you taught me the importance of honesty and the gift in speaking my truth. You are my inspiration to helping women and teen girls. I am dedicating this book, my coaching business and my journey to serve to you. Thank you for teaching me to authentically seek the beauty in others. Thank you for teaching me how to remain true to myself. I have so much gratitude to you for modeling radical love in the way you loved me.

Mom, you are a true testament on how to love a daughter. If I am half the woman you are, than I am woman enough!

Contents

Foreword

Every woman needs a friend, a confidant and a cheerleader who wants nothing more than to celebrate her successes and encourage her dreams. In her delightfully warm and deeply engaging new book, Radical Love – Your Path to Freedom and Bliss, Melanie Foote-Davis provides a blueprint for discovering a life of transformative love and powerful acceptance. Found, within the pages of this work, is a wealth of heart-felt knowledge, wisdom and practical information to help women embrace the power of love for self and the possibilities of abundant and vibrant life.

Nearly a decade ago, I had the good fortune to meet Melanie and since then, I have been a beneficiary of both a coaching relationship and a meaningful friendship. Both relationships have been blessings in my life and now you are on the receiving end of her genuine and profound plan to enhance the life you are living. You now possess a powerful weapon to battle for the life you deserve. So, go for it!

In Radical Love, Melanie is a masterful coach and trusted voice of encouragement and inspiration. Just by picking up this book you have demonstrated that you are ready to ask yourself the serious questions and to do the transformational work necessary to achieve the abundant life you desire. As you take this guided journey to self-discovery, Melanie provides challenging wisdom lessons that steer her readers into a new life of freedom, joy and yes, radical love and bliss.

With great integrity and an abundance of love, Melanie offers meaningful information for all women, regardless of where they may find themselves on their life's journey. She skillfully offers women another paradigm – a new way to embrace themselves completely, lovingly and without judgement. This is not a book about becoming perfect, but it is about honesty, becoming real and telling the truth. Melanie motivates her reader to remove the masks, to step outside of the shadows and to show up in life! Her message lets us know that our past is gone and a wonderful life awaits us RIGHT NOW!!

Any woman who has ever questioned her own self-worth, inherent value or purpose in life will gain significant insight and knowledge from this reading. Each chapter provides powerful truth lessons that lead to effective action. For any sister who is ready to manifest change in her life, Melanie provides a comprehensive, radical and life-altering plan.

Melanie reminds women who are ready for significant and lasting change that the search for meaning requires a deeper look at motivations and patterns of behavior. Radical Love - Your Path to Freedom and Bliss teaches that reflection, honesty and determination are the keys to liberation and actualization. Georgia O'Keefe, famed American artist states, "I feel that there is something unexplored about women that only a woman can explore." Melanie becomes our guide and coach as we explore and journey together.

Melanie's main objective is to enhance and improve women's lives. She leads us into better versions of ourselves through sound reasoning, a depth of spiritual insight and good old common sense. The gift Melanie offers is tried and true wisdom and practical tools for the journey to self-acceptance and radical love. Are you ready to take the challenge to live a life where radical self-love prevails? If so, don't hesitate another moment. Give this gift to yourself because you deserve it. You won't be disappointed!

Introduction

Congratulations! I am so proud of you for taking steps to fill your heart and soul with love. I am absolutely thrilled to share this space with you. The mere fact that you are here means that you are committed to investing in personal time with one of the most amazing people you know. That person is YOU. I honor you for taking that step. Please know there are endless possibilities available to you from this moment on.

We all have a story. I don't know yours, but my intuition tells me that chapters in my story resonate with yours in some small way. My series of events are different from yours. My feelings and emotions may be similar to that which you have experienced. I want you to know that you are not alone although you may sometimes feel that way. My hope is that my sharing will support you in recreating the parts of your story that has been holding you back. My hope is that you to rewrite your story in a way that fills your life's cup with wins that bring you an abundance of joy and fulfillment. The operative word here is abundance. Notice I didn't say a little joy and fulfillment. I said abundance. Fill your cup to the point of overflow. Give from that abundant space.

Here's why I chose to share. My closet was filled with masks. I had a mask for every occasion. One mask said that I was confident. Another mask said that I had it all together. I owned a, 'you can count on me to listen' 24 hours a day, 7 days a week, and 365 days a year mask for friends, family and even colleagues. I was a night owl. Believe it or not, I took calls at 3:00 am. I never wanted anyone to feel like I wasn't there if and when they needed a sounding board. So I created an atmosphere for others that said 'your emergency was also my emergency', even if I was actually sleeping. Go figure.

Some believed that my life was fabulous. On some level, they were correct. Amazing things are happening in my life. I have an incredible relationship with my daughter. I am blessed to have a supportive husband and a very loving family. God placed beautifully gifted and caring souls on my path. I have a strong faith in God. I am blessed beyond measure. I know that sounds cliché, but that is how I honestly feel....Blessed. My needs are met.

As I write this I am reminded of a conversation with a former colleague. For the sake of this conversation, we'll call her Sherry. She was venting and sharing her current circumstances. Sherry observed the way that my family responded to each other. We greet with hugs, especially my mom. We offer moral support for things that may seem insignificant to others. My family didn't wait for weddings and funerals to connect. My sisters and cousins hung out with each other just because, no occasion necessary.

She finished venting. She paused. Of course, I'm paraphrasing because it would be fake for me pretend that I remember her exact words. She looked at me and said something along the lines of 'You probably wouldn't understand what I'm going through because your life is perfect. Your family doesn't have struggles like this. You're always there for each other.'

That conversation was both shocking and uncomfortable to hear. Her comment shed light on the impact that my masks can have on others. It showed me that I must be mindful of what I am modeling. It is important to be authentic. Our public persona may be empowering. But, it may also be discouraging when others can only see one dimension of your life. Albeit unintentional, it can contribute to people feeling disconnected to you because it feels like what you have is too far for them to reach. I am not saying that we should not use discretion in terms of how much we expose. Some things are meant to remain private. However, I never considered the possibility of someone else viewing my family's relationship as perfect. Some may experience that as difficult to relate to and even unattainable. The thought of that saddened me.

Believing that my life was perfect couldn't have been further from my truth. My reality was that occasionally I didn't know whether I was coming or going. I wasn't confident enough to ask for the appropriate fees for my services. I was the Queen of discount. That cost me. I discounted my way into debt. There were days when I wasn't sure how I would pay my bills yet I volunteered to pick up the tab at dinner.

I indulged in more toxic dating relationships than I care to admit. I honestly don't enjoy seeing others in pain. Therefore, I wanted everyone around me to be happy. The thought of me not being available to help someone was inconceivable to me. I was so busy trying to be everything to everyone else. I experienced times when I was so determined to be available to others that I failed to be here, there or anywhere else for me.

I had a great support system in place. I had too much pride to ask for help. Meanwhile, I was falling apart. It became difficult to make simple decisions. I began to second guess my self-worth, my work and everything I was doing or had ever done. I began to reflect on my entire life. Actually, I was not really viewing my entire life. The only aspects of my life visible to me were my mistakes, my short-comings and the ways that I had fallen short. That led me to series of negative internal dialogue, shame, blame and guilt. It wasn't un-til I felt like I was losing my sense of self that I began to slow down. I mean that literally. I felt like a part of me was dying inside. I did my best to make sense of what was happening. I looked for ways to justify why I should continue on this path of self-destruction.

I methodically began each day clothed in my masks, ended many nights with my pillow drenched in tears. Time passed. Peace of mind seemed to be nowhere within my reach.

Theoretically I knew God loved me. Theoretically I knew that God is omnipresent. Seriously, I was really too engulfed in my own self-in-duced suffering to embody that reality. My mind was too cluttered to hear God speak or to feel his presence. I was fully committed to the perception of being in control, yet I was not in control at all. The proverbial "S" on my chest was growing as I continued to hold my superwoman mask with all my might. I failed to see that the most important action was not for me to hold, but to willingly let go. Let me say that differently. I was holding on so tightly to everything that was holding me back from being my best self. As long as my hands were full of that which was not good for me, I had no free hands to reach for what would ultimately set me free. I was imprisoned within my own mind.

By the way, Superwoman is not real. She doesn't exist at least not in the way we define her. I have a request if you choose to embrace that title of Superwoman. My request is that you consider retiring her. Ok so maybe retiring her feels like too much for you right now. Maybe you see your superwoman as your badge of honor. Maybe some part of you secretly enjoys people acknowledging you for doing so much. Are you seeking validation in that? Will you at least give your superwoman permission to ask for and accept support? Remember, I needed to move out of my own way and surrender. I needed to let God lead my path. I encourage you to do the same.

Truth be told, a part of me enjoyed having others lean on me. After all, contribution is one of my values. I thoroughly enjoyed giving. I enjoyed pouring love into their cups. I felt necessary and useful. I felt like it gave me purpose. I felt like, "Hey that's the least I can do. They are worth it, right?"

I failed to realize that I too had value. I failed to acknowledge that my own life was worth pouring into. I ultimately exhausted my personal resources. Self-care is essential to our overall health. It is important to fill my cup first and pour from the overflow. It was imperative for me to nurture my physical, spiritual, emotional and financial needs. The only thing I had left were vapors…fumes. My cup was empty. I was trying to pour from an empty cup. How is that even possible? How could I give anything from a depleted place? Guess what? I was giving from my leftovers. My daughter, my friends, my clients were all getting my leftovers. Weren't they worthy of more? Wasn't I worthy of more? Aren't you worthy of more?

Does any of this sound familiar to you? Does this sound like I'm preparing to tell your story? Well I am not. I couldn't possibly do your story justice; not the way that you can. You are the best candidate to tell your story in the way that you want it told.

So here is the thing. Let's take time to clear up a few things before either of us approaches the path to storytelling. It would be really interesting to share my journey in a way that makes others feel sorry for me. I could stand in the victim's perspective. I could totally play the victim. I could host a grand red carpet event called *Girl Let Me Tell You Soiree.* I could send out an E-Blast and a social media campaign inviting every woman who has experienced pain, felt taken advantage of, been heartbroken, etc. We could play games called, *"Humph… If* You *Think That's Bad"* and *"Let Me Tell You What They Did to Me."* The swag bags would consist of matches to burn photos of our ex-offenders, tissues and cosmetics to refresh our make-up after we share a good ugly cry. You know there is nothing like a good ugly cry with your girlfriends. But that's not why I'm here. There is no room for me to play the victim. It won't do you any good either.

I shared that brief synopsis only to let you know that I can empathize with you. Essentially, I am here to celebrate you. I am here to reaffirm your personal power. I am here to remind you that you will have disappointments. You will make both wise and unwise choices. People will not show up for you in the way that you want them to. My question for you is how will you show up for you?

The beauty of it is that your power is in your response to it all. You have the power to choose how you will respond to each experience. We are co-creator of our life stories. We actively participate in every second of our lives. Now I'm not talking about those moments when someone had absolutely no control, like abuse, muggings etc. They are traumatic and often powerless moments. Those are actual times when the term victim is appropriate.

I am talking about the toxic relationships we choose. I am talking about our financial choices. I am talking about the people and behaviors we invite into our space. You know like when we see crazy coming and we wall towards it instead of crossing the street. I am talking about the times we sign up for additional responsibilities when there is no more room on our calendar for the ones we already said yes to. These moments are within our control.

Now that we have established that we co-create our own realities. This is the moment when you can choose to create a new ending to your story. It is time to take full power and control of your destiny.

This is what I want you to do. Yes, I know. We haven't gotten to the first chapter yet and I'm already giving you an assignment. Yes. I am. Why? I love you just that much. I am serious about you creating the life you want. This moment is the only time in which we have control. Let's seize the moment. No worries. We're going to take baby steps. We are on this journey together. I am right here with you. Are you ready? Let's go! Grab yourself some water to hydrate, a pen and a timer. I'll wait for your return.

Welcome back Beautiful! Place your hand on your heart. I encourage you to take a deep breath. Inhale love. Exhale. Inhale kindness. Exhale. Inhale peace. Exhale. Inhale joy. Exhale. Let's do that one more time. Exhale. Ahhh…. Doesn't that feel good? Your body should be relaxing a bit more. You breathed in love, kindness, peace and joy for you. You exhaled love, kindness, peace and joy back out into the universe.

Read the instructions before you set your timer. Lay this book aside. Get in a comfortable position. Close your eyes and continue to inhale and exhale slowly. Imagine how you want your story to end. Imagine what your amazing future. What are you see? What does your future smell like? What do you hear? How does your future feel? What is your posture? Who is with you? See it in full color. Continue to imagine for at least two minutes. When the timer goes off, slowly open your eyes. Now take whatever it is that you just imagined and write it down as quickly as you can.

Write down what you just envisioned. This is not a time to be perfect. Don't concern yourself with grammar or anything. It may be blurred or you may see it clearly. Write whatever you saw, heard or tasted without judgement. Draw it out if that works best for you. Simply capture the vision. You can always come back to it later as you see more. This is between you and God.

_____

_____

_____

_____

_____

_____

_____

_____

_____

_____

Great job!! Give yourself a big hug.

Essential Keys to Love Your Way through This Guide:
This is a proactive guide. This requires your energy input. Are you ready to experience radical love? Great! I knew you would say yes. Your life is waiting for you. Let's get busy with filling your cup with all of the delicious and juicy goodness that life has available to you.

Statistics show that new habits are formed over a 21-day period. For the next 21 days I am encouraging you to be a willing vessel. Identify a quiet place to reflect and connect with God or your higher being. I challenge you to explore opportunities to intentionally fill your life's cup with love. In this case I am speaking of love for you. I will share food for thought each day. This is not going to be comfortable. I will challenge you to reach into the crevices of your soul. Here's the truth. You are not growing when you are too comfortable any way. Growth happens when you stretch and expand beyond the place of knowing. Spend time reflecting. Then respond to the journaling assignments. Make the commitment to do the work. Practice the new behaviors. This isn't about perfection. It is about developing new habits that serve you.

The truth will set you free is not just another aphorism. It is a fact of life. Give yourself the gift of freedom by being as honest as possible. Your breakthrough is on the other side of that honesty. Let me be transparent. I am not asking more of you than I ask of myself. I also get stuck and challenged with doing my own work. Know that I am right here pressing through with you. I am holding a space in my heart for you. We are riding this love train together.

Use the blank pages at the end of the assignment to release whatever God has for you in that particular area of your life. I encourage you to write your daily celebrations in this journal as well. Find something to celebrate on a consistent basis. You are worth the acknowledgment. Every step forward equals progress. This is about you. Walk through this at the pace that works best for you. That means when you feel led to go back and review, do so. There is nothing here but love for you. There may be more learning and opportunity for you in that area. Embrace it. Be gracious. It may take you more than 21 days. So what? The most important your honor yourself by nurturing your needs each day.

I encourage you not to grow alone. We all need the support of a community. I lean heavily on my community for accountability and encouragement. Identify an accountability partner. Share this opportunity with a friend. You can support each other over the next 21 days. Be open to what will become of this partnership. It may deepen your relationship in ways you never imagined. Wouldn't that be awesome?!!!

Celebrate the Beauty of You

The celebration of beauty is an invitation to ask your soul every day,
'mind if I join you'
~Anonymous
The more you praise and celebrate your life, the more there is in life
to celebrate.
Oprah Winfrey

Celebrate what you want to see more of. Thomas J. Peters

While we are living in the present, we must celebrate life every day,
knowing that we are becoming history with every work, every ac-
tion, every deed.
Mattie Stepanek

Celebrate the happiness that friends are always giving, make every
day a holiday and celebrate just living! Amanda Bradley

Stop worrying about the potholes in the road and celebrate the journey! Barbara Hoffman

Have you noticed how much you celebrate and encourage babies? As a child is developing her motor skills, you champion her along the way. You encourage her first everything; the first time she rolls over, the first time she sits up alone, her first step, her first word and her first day of school.

I remember my daughter's first word. She said, "Hat." You would've thought I had won the lottery. I called my mother into the room to hear it. I looked at Trinity, my daughter. I said, "Baby, say hat." She said, "Hat". We nearly jumped through the roof. I began to make phone calls to share the good news.

What did you notice about that example? Did I wait until my daughter was speaking in complete sentences before celebrating her? No, I did not. Did I say, "Well she only spoke one word?" No, I did not.

So what makes us do that to ourselves? Societal standards and external conditions have taught us many things that ultimately destroy our well-being. We have been conditioned to delay our own acknowledgement. To do so may be indicative of conceit. Then we have to wait for external acknowledgement to celebrate. Really?!! Whose bright idea was that? Denying the opportunity to celebrate on our own behalf is another form of bondage. Where is the liberation in that? It is the equivalent of placing a sign up with flashing red lights "No personal joy allowed".

I'm not a sports aficionado. However, I don't need to be to notice the celebrations that occur at games. Let's take a few lessons from athletes and their fans. In football the fans cheer each time their team advances towards the end zone. The fans celebrate every completed pass. The fans celebrate the touchdown even when the team is losing. The fans do not wait until they win the game to cele- brate. The players dance in the end zone even if they are losing by eighteen points. The fans applaud with great enthusiasm. They are in expectation of a big win. Yet they choose to acknowledge small wins throughout the process.

Every step of your journey is worth acknowledgment too. When was the last time you acknowledged small wins throughout your day? How often do you celebrate the achievement of others?

_____

_____

Have you ever felt that you have to wait for something big to happen before it's appropriate to celebrate? Why is that? Every breath we take is worth celebrating. Every step you take towards moving forward is worth celebrating. There is no need to wait to enjoy your life. Why are you waiting for the grand finale to get your applause? I say, let's dance our way to the goal.

I usually begin my coaching calls with celebrations. Sometimes clients come to the call believing they have no reason to celebrate. During our time together they discover that they are minimizing their own accomplishments. We have a celebration party during the session. I literally skip or do the cabbage patch on their behalf. Yes, I said cabbage patch. I don't know new dances.

Quick story:

I was shopping in Office Depot one afternoon. My phone rang. My friend was calling to share a major accomplishment. I was so excited for her. I started doing the cabbage patch right there in the aisle of Office Depot. My arms were swaying and rotating across my chest. I was saying Whoohoo,Whoohoo. An employee was walking by and saw me. I didn't see him because I was in the midst of my groove. Then I heard a man's voice say, "Aww.....break it down." My friend, Maya could hear him through the phone too. We all laughed.

The beauty of that story is by her calling to celebrate her win led to a complete stranger having a joyous moment as well. Isn't that awesome? I can still see myself dancing. The visual of me doing the cabbage patch continues to amuse me. It brings me joy. You're probably laughing at the image in your head too. Aren't you? LOL.

I'm not sure if you noticed. The party for you is already happening. The very first sentence in this book began in celebration of you. I said, "Congratulations! I am so proud of you for taking steps to fill your heart and soul with love." I really mean that.

It's your turn. Find something that you can celebrate in this moment. Place your hand over your heart. Breathe love in deeply. Exhale slowly. Breathe in again. Exhale slowly. Reflect on events of this past week. Go to your heart, not your head. In other words try not to think. Instead tap into the feeling of single moments. Remember that it doesn't have to be major. Every step is worth acknowledging. Keep it sweet. Keep it simple. Find a reason to have a personal dance party right now. Go ahead I dare you.

What transpired for you this week that felt really good inside? Did you offer a kind word to someone? Did you receive a compliment or acknowledgement? Did you find your happy place and sing in the car? Did you stop dead in your tracks when you noticed a beautiful woman and realized that was your own reflection? Take a moment to love the skin you're in. You are worth celebrating at any stage, any shade, any size and any age.

Radical ways to fill your love cup with celebrations:

- Be your own best friend
- See each day as a new opportunity to embrace the best life has to offer
- Change the way you see yourself. See your greatness, your beauty and your power.
- Celebrate all of you. Love your curves, your eyes,
- Dance in celebration of you. You're worth the party. You are the prize!!!
- Find something to be proud of daily. Write it down.
- Think of a time when you were happy, joyful or fulfilled.
- Acknowledge at least one great quality you possess. Choose one that helps you feel powerful. Write it down. Place it in your mirror to remind you of your awesomeness.
- Celebrate others. Be happy for others when they experience joy.
- Place your hand over your heart. Complete these statements. I Am Seen. I Am Heard. I Am Worthy. I Am Enough. I Am Loved.

Today I celebrate.....

_____

_____

_____

(Aha Moments) Today I discovered....

_____

_____

_____

_____

I felt great when......

_____

_____

_____

_____

_____

Mind Your Thoughts

You are listening to your own thoughts even when no one else is tuned in. Mind your thoughts.
Melanie Foote-Davis

You can hear everything you are thinking.
Melanie Foote-Davis

Let's spend a little time with the conversations we have in our head. It is important that we discuss our mindset before we can fully step into new behaviors. Why? Your actions are preceded by thoughts. Your mind is a powerful tool. How you choose to utilize this tool is totally based on BS. Relax. I am not cursing at you. I am referring to your **Belief System.** Information has been fed to you since birth. Based on what you heard, what you observed and how you processed it influenced your view of the world.

Think back to past conversations. See it as the soundtrack of your beliefs. They were seeping into your subconscious. Now think about what you observed. Or better yet, think about your perception of what you observed. Your observation was guided by what you heard playing in the background. It was shaped by the conversations you heard growing up, the television programs you watched and the books you read.

Studies reveal that a human being has approximately sixty thousand thoughts per day. Ninety percent of those are repetitive thoughts from the day before. Eighty percent of our thoughts are negative. If eighty percent of our thoughts are negative then how does that affect our overall well-being?

Pierre Teilhard de Chardin says, "We are not human beings having a spiritual experience. We are spiritual beings having a human experience." Our bodies respond to our thoughts, our feelings and our actions. It is often referred to as mind-body connection. Jennifer Hawthorne of Chicken Soup for the Woman's Soul says this, "If you're tired physically, it's hard to think clearly. On the other hand, if you've been using your mind doing mental work all day, you're likely to feel the effects physically, too.

It is imperative that you mind your thoughts. Remember that we have repetitive negative thoughts. Listen to your internal dialogue. Are your thoughts beginning to sound like someone hit the repeat button on your life's playlist? Are you telling the same old stories? What will I hear if I had the ability to turn up the volume on your thoughts? Will I hear phrases like this?

"If I hadn't_____I would be _____ by now."
"I knew I shouldn't have listened to ...."
"I can't_____ because...."
"I'm not like (insert name here).
"I don't have _____like (insert name)."

If so, STOP IT! Stop it right now. I told you earlier that this is your time to write a new ending to your story. Repetitive thoughts like "If I hadn't" "should", "can't" complaining thoughts, worry or comparison are all depleting your energy. They also drain the energy of those listening to you. It will literally suck the life out of you. I am serious about this. It may cause you to question your self-worth. It may physically show up in your body in the form of fatigue or illness. Remember, it is mind-body connection. That only gives you another thing to whine, complain or worry about. Shift your thought pattern when and if you notice this dialogue in your head. What gets your energy gets you.

It is equally important to pay close attention to the conversations around you as well. You must mind your mental noise. That mental head trash hinders our ability to receive the love, joy and peace you so desperately desire.

How do you acquire the proverbial peace? You get there by quieting your mind, acknowledging what you are experiencing and choosing to make the mental shift. The joy you want comes from within. The love you want comes from within. But you must choose it. It will in turn choose you.

Wikipedia describes inner peace as Inner peace (or peace of mind) refers to a state of being mentally and spiritually at peace, with enough knowledge and understanding to keep oneself strong in the face of discord or stress. Being "at peace" is considered by many to be healthy (homeostasis) and the opposite of being stressed or anxious. Peace of mind is generally associated with bliss, happiness and contentment.

Consider the way you approach a new day. The way that you begin your day can set the tone for the remainder of your day. The power of your thoughts lies within where you choose to place your energy and your focus.

Let's say you get out of bed. You stump your toe. Is your response, "Oh man! It's going to be one of those days." Or do you say, "Ouch!" and move forward with getting your day started? Both options are personal choices. Which one will you choose?

What is the first thing that you think as you rise? Are you waking up with gratitude? Does your day begin with divine connection? Are you logging onto the computer to check email or social media within the first hour of the day? Are you passively listening to the news as you dress?

Becoming mindful of the way you begin your day is key. Let's pretend that you're listening for traffic updates and the weather forecast. Unfortunately, the majority of reports while you wait for traffic and weather are deficit based. You are passively listening to stories about shootings, political bullies, social injustice, the struggling economy, blah, blah, blah. How depressing is that?

Is it important for me to be aware of the state of the world? Absolutely! One of the ways that I take care of myself is by choosing what, how and when I absorb this content. I choose not to start my day with tragic news. I can look it up later online when my mind is ready to ingest it. Realistically, it is news because it's already happened. It is beyond my control. My hearing doesn't reverse what has already occurred. That is not being insensitive. This is being aware of what I do and do not have the power to control.

I choose to begin my day with God. I am grateful for another day and another opportunity to serve. I intentionally ask, "How may I serve today?" I ask God to use me to be a blessing to someone else today. Sometimes, I listen to inspirational videos or podcasts while I get dress. Other days, I may reflect on schedule and think of healthy ways to approach each task.

What does this have to do with minding your thoughts? It has a great deal to do with minding your thoughts. Hearing something repeatedly can lead to believing that it is true for you. What will you begin to believe when you are surrounded by conversations of lack? You may buy into the belief that there is not enough of anything for you. You may believe:

- All politicians are corrupt.
- You have to settle for a career you no longer enjoy because there aren't enough jobs.

- You aren't safe in certain neighborhoods.
- All shootings are gang-related.

That can lead you to a hopeless and depleted place. Thoughts of hopelessness will keep you stuck in the land of depletion.

I encourage you to believe that there is more for you. We serve a God of abundance. You must change the way you see the world. View it from a place of curiosity and possibility. Your path to freedom is depending on you making a shift in your thinking.
This is what is true.

- Some politicians are good people with great intentions to help their constituents.
- The career you want is available to you.
- There are loving people in every neighborhood with no desire to harm you.
- Joy and fulfillment is available to you. You must believe it is possible for it to manifest in your life.

It is imperative that you mind your thoughts. There is power in your intention. Your intentions start within. Be very careful with getting clear about your intentions. Become as specific as you can about it. It is not just about what you want or where you want to go. It is more important to tune into your energy or belief of the possibility of it manifesting in your life.

You must be connected to it on a soul level. You can quote scriptures and affirmations ten times a day. They are mere words better left unspoken when your mouth and your thoughts are in two separate conversations. There is more power in the energy behind the thought than the words. What you believe and what you speak must be in alignment. You may say things like:

"I am prosperous."
"God is my source and my supplier."
"All things are possible with God"

Immediately after you say that, your thoughts are:

"I don't know how I'm going to pay my mortgage this month."
"I can't afford..."
"I don't have the money for ..."

Does that sound like abundance to you? No. It is coming from a consciousness of lack. You believe that you are experiencing a deficiency. Whatever you believe is what will manifest in your life. You are co-creating it based on your energy level in that moment. Pay close attention to what you are thinking and the feeling associated with that thought. What gets your attention gets you!!!

Think in terms of what you want. Typically if I ask a client what she wants, she responds with what she doesn't want. Therefore when I ask questions based on desires, she speaks from a place of lack because that's where her emotions are. She is focused on the perceived deficiencies in her life.
To believe something is possible for you starts with you actually believing that it's possible even when the evidence of it is invisible.

Be mindful of your thoughts from this point on. None of us are exempt from having an off day. It takes intentional effort to master this mindset. Practice it daily. Notice that I didn't say perfect it. I said practice. Be mindful of your internal conversations. Pay close attention to the people within your circle of influence.

You may already be aligned with prosperity and abundance mind-set. If that's the case, let me pause to celebrate you. This chapter can simply serve as a refresher for you. This is a great time for you to share your transition from lack to abundance with friends and family. You can be a great support to them.

Mind your thoughts with your family, friends and colleagues. What are you talking about? Pay attention to your offline and online conversations. Who do you follow on social media? What is their mindset? Again, what are you passively hearing or absorbing into your subconscious?

Which side of the chart shows up in your thoughts or your conversations most often? Focus on which connections and behaviors will bring you closer to your freedom. Your relationships carry a lot weight. We will discuss your relationships later in chapter 6.

Jim Rohn says, "You are the average of the five people you spend the most time with." I want to be very clear that you spend all of your time with yourself. So let's make that six people so that you are fully aware that you matter as well. Think about the five people to spend the most time with. Time spent is not limited to physical time together in person. It includes, phone conversations, text messages, social media engagement, etc .

List your five people here.

1. _____
2. _____
3. _____
4. _____
5. _____

Look at the Asset Based and Deficit Based chart. Pay attention to which people consistently land on the asset based chart. They are the people who add value to your life. It may be time for you to make new agreements with those who consistently land on the deficit based chart. Don't forget to include where your behaviors are landing on this chart as well. Make the necessary adjustments to begin to create a life of freedom and bliss.

Asset Based Attitudes/Behaviors		Asset Based Conversations
Acceptance	Fun	I Am
Achievement	Free spirit	I enjoy
Acknowledg-	Giving	I have
ment	Gratitude	I love
Adventurous	Inspirational	I win
Celebratory	Joyful	
Compliment	Optimistic	
Confident	Solution Oriented	
Encouragement	Supportive	
Expectancy		
Deficit Based Attitudes/Behaviors		Deficit Based Conversations
Comparison	Gossip	I should
Complaint	Judgmental Negative	I can't
Complacent	Pessimistic	I wish
Condescend	Rejection	If only I had...
Criticize	Restricted/Confined	The only reason I
Doubt/Worry	Shame	haven't is...
Drama magnet	Whiny	They did __ to me
Entitlement		

I have something else for you to consider. If you consistently spend a great deal of time following specific people online via, blogs, social media, podcasts and YouTube, consider that as time spent. Include the people you follow but may not engage or interact with.

For example, if you read xyz blog a blog or follow on social media but you never comment, share or repost. Remember, we are talking about minding your thoughts. Believe or not, they have a tremendous impact on your thinking. You are compelled to tune into what they are doing or what they are sharing for a reason.

Who are they? List their names or the websites below.

1._____

2. _____

3. _____

4. _____

5. _____

What is that reason for you?

_____

_____

How do you feel when you are reading their commentary or listening to them?

_____

_____

How many hours a week are you tuned in to what they are sharing?

_____

What is it about them that pulls you in?

_____

_____

Take time to really check in with yourself to see what comes up for you.

Radical Ways to Mind Your Thoughts:

- Be mindful of the way you begin and end your day.
- Be intentional about what you passively listen to as you fall asleep. (The artificial lights from technology affect our sleep. I encourage you to turn off the television and other electronic devices.)
- End each day with gratitude.
- Rest with an expectation of wonderful new possibilities of tomorrow. Enjoy your restful nights.

Today I celebrate.....

_____

_____

_____

Today I discovered....

_____

_____

_____

_____

I felt great when......

_____

_____

_____

_____

Live Abundantly

Many of us think of money when we hear the words abundance, prosperity or wealth. The truth is that abundance, wealth and prosperity is not limited to money or material things. There is a wealth of health, love, fun, food, entertainment, time and freedom. The list is endless. Let's look at it from another perspective. What if we simplified it? Try looking at it this way.

Abundance = large quantity or plentiful
Wealth = means or resources
Prosper = grow, flourish, thrive or succeed

Answer the following without using money as your answer.

1. What would you like to have in large quantities?

_____

_____

2. What means or resources would you like access to?

_____

_____

3. In what areas of your life would you like to grow or succeed?

_____

_____

Now put them all together here by filling in the blanks. Place your answer to #1 in the space below.

I am open to acquiring an abundance of _____

_____.

Place your answer to #2 in the space below.

I am open to receiving a wealth of _____

_____

Place your answer to #3 in the space below.

My life is prospering as I speak in the following areas _____

_____

.

Great job! Now take a deep breath. Place your hand over your heart. Read each sentence out loud with feeling. Repeat this step three times. Exhale. Doesn't that feel amazing? If you are not beginning to feel great energy vibrating through your body then you are probably resisting the possibility of experiencing abundance. Relax. You are not alone. We talked earlier about your belief system. We also talked about your mindset. It takes time to shift completely into the consciousness of abundance. I am proud of you for making the attempt. That alone is progress. You didn't get to where you are overnight. You won't get to where you want to be overnight.   Keep practicing. It will begin to become a way of life for you. Practice until you embody it and feel it within your being.

Let's explore a bit more. What types of conversations are you engaging with family, friends and colleagues? Shift your focus to abundance whenever you find your thoughts or energy sinking into a space of lack or deficit based thinking.

Think about the conversations you may have heard during childhood. Take a look at money conversations in which you were exposed. What did your parents or guardians say about wealth or money? Did you ever hear anyone arguing about money? Did you hear things like, *"we can't afford"* or *"money doesn't grow on trees"*?

Think about what you heard or read within the past week. Consider online and offline conversations. Think of dialogue that involved wishing for something or thoughts of lack.. Other thoughts that may cause you to live in lack are:

"Money changes you."
"Money is the root of all evil."
"The rich get richer and the poor get poorer."
"More money, more problems"
"It is better to give than receive."
"She's changed since she started earning more money."

What are your money stories or beliefs about wealthy people or people with more access than you? _____
_____

You may have difficulty receiving if your money story or belief system about having plenty is that it is better to give than to receive. This discomfort with receiving is not limited to money. If this sounds like you than you may also be uncomfortable, accepting any and all gifts, including compliments, rewards or acknowledgement. There is some judgment, shame or guilt about having access to something that others don't' currently have. If this resonates with you then I encourage you to release that burden of guilt now.

Women who view access to resources as bad are often hesitant to ask for what she wants or what she needs. She often settles for less than she desires. Overtime that has a huge impact on her perception of her personal value, self-confidence and self-worth. Or she may live on the other side of the spectrum over-compensating, overachieving, over-indulging, over-spending, confrontational, defensive and always having something to prove. Both sides of the spectrum leads to the same thing; the absence of peace, freedom and bliss.

We serve a God of abundance. That means there is more than enough for everyone. You don't have to do without so that others may have. Now I agree that it may or may not be currently distributed well. Even that is rooted in a belief in lack. For example, Lack consciousness in playing full out when one person believes that sharing what she has with another means there won't be enough left for her. This can be true of anyone, even those with ample resources. It is not about what a person does or does not have. It is about the mindset associated with that particular resource. I am in no way saying that you must give without discernment. It is important for us to be good stewards of what we've been blessed with.

I am the youngest of eight children. My parents had children over a twenty-one year timeframe. Therefore, my siblings are 7-21 years older than me. That means by the time I was six or seven years old, most of my siblings had moved out of my parent's home. With that said, my life experiences with my parents are vastly different than my siblings. My parents are by no means wealthy. However, money management is one of my mother's many gifts. I had access to simple luxuries that my siblings did not. I had my own bedroom. I had a television in my room. We took vacations. I had plenty of clothes. Unlike some of my peers, I could go for weeks without repeating the same outfit. I didn't ask for much. But, I have no memory of my parents ever saying to me that they couldn't afford anything I requested. I wanted to go to modeling school. My parents enrolled me without hesitation. My mother adjusted her schedule to drive approximately 160 miles roundtrip for weeks. I wanted to spend a couple of weeks.in Munich, Germany visiting my friend Carmen from modeling school. My parents were making plans for me to go. My summer plans in Germany we altered because I learned that I was receiving an unexpected blessing, my daughter Trinity. Whew! Talk about a shift in priorities.

I observed very intentional behaviors as it relates to finances. My mother habitually tithed 10% of earnings before anything else. She paid bills on time. She would literally drive to the merchant to pay in person to ensure they received it. Honoring financial commitments is a huge value for her. Both of my parents are generous and freely shared their resources. They gave of their time, money and talents to others. They modeled an attitude of gratitude. I am so grateful to have witnessed that.

Today I feel extremely blessed to have had access to simple luxuries that may not have been available to my siblings or to my peers. Here the thing. As a child and well into my adult life, I was confused about these blessings. I wasn't sure how to find joy in my access to experiences and tangible items. I lived in a state of guilt and shame for being smart, having more clothes, longer hair and frequent weekend getaways. Some of my peers wouldn't play with me or said hurtful things to me about my clothes. During my high school years, I received prank phone calls and threats of being jumped at school the next day. They showed no mercy even while I was pregnant. I will never forget one caller who said, "I will F#@& a pregnant girl up!" Yikes! Caller ID didn't exist. To this day, I do not know who made those phone calls. They may actually be a follower on Facebook. At this stage in my life it no longer has power over me. I heard things like, "You think you're cute because you have long hair." You think you're better than everyone else." "You think you can dress better than us."

I know they are worse things in life. Tell that to a hormonal teenager. I simply did not know how to process that at the time. I didn't know how to tell my mother without getting someone in trouble. My desire wasn't to get anyone in trouble. I simply wanted it to stop. I wanted to be accepted. I didn't feel like it was fair to be treated badly simply because my circumstances were different from theirs.

I was twenty years old. I remember sitting in the bedroom of my first apartment. I was going through some boxes. I found my old diary. Reading my thoughts from my childhood was so depressing. I remember ripping the pages out and destroying them. I never ever wanted to read them again. It was painful because the one person who treated me badly that I could identity was someone I loved dearly.

You may ask, why does any of this matter? You may be wondering what any of this has to do with love, freedom, bliss or living abundantly. It has everything to do with it. So let's fast forward to years later. I am listening to a Suze Orman cassette tape in my car. Suze was doing a "money memories" exercise. Something was happening to my body. I remember feeling tight and constricted. I could barely swallow from the golf ball in my throat. My vison was impaired from the water in my eyes. I don't recall how much further I needed to drive. I do remember feeling like something inside was forcing its way out of me. I made it home safely at the mercy of a wing and a prayer.

Have you heard that when you know better you do better? I knew how to manage money. I knew how to generate consistent income. For the life of me, I just couldn't understand why I continued to leave money on the table when doing business. I knew how to create a budget or spending plan. I knew how to live within my means. Yet, I didn't. I was on a vicious cycle of spending more than I earned.

I didn't know it at the time but I was experiencing my first abundance breakthrough in my car. I grabbed a notebook and a pen.

I began to write what was coming up for me. I discovered that I was sabotaging my own success. It was in that very moment that I learned that I had self-judgment. I processed my childhood experiences to mean that I was not destined to have too much of anything without painful consequences. Let me be clear. I did not say that was true. That was simply how I processed my childhood experiences. My abundance belief was that **people I love will reject me when and if I have more.**

Whew! Let me take a moment to exhale. That was huge. It is not just any one would reject me. It is people that I love. That made it personal and intimate. My body tightened as I shared that. I have only shared that with a select group of people in my inner circle with whom I feel safe. What I know for sure is that I needed to share that with you. Someone whom I may never meet needed to read that.

Let me tell you how that showed up in my life. I had an unconscious set point for access in all areas of my life. I refused tips from clients in cosmetology school. I subconsciously let go of money when I reached a certain income level. I manifested my first home through creative visualization, and then I let it go in bankruptcy.

My husband Sean adores me. Can you guess what I did? I used to minimize the joy in my marriage whenever I was talking to friends or acquaintances who were unhappy in their relationships. Do you see the pattern here? I subconsciously avoided all paths to freedom and bliss even within my own marriage. Well that's not necessarily true. I didn't completely avoid access to paths to freedom and bliss. I subconsciously chose alternate paths when "happy" hung around too long. I felt guilty for feeling happy and enjoying dates with my husband. Sometimes I even created tension in our relationship by nitpicking. I was afraid to live in the proverbial healthy and happy marriage for long period of time. I shared this discovery with my friend Miki. She brought something very important to my attention. Not only was I sabotaging my freedom, I was dishonest. Minimizing my joy was anything but truthful. There is no peace in dishonesty. It shows a lack of integrity. It is out of alignment with abundance.

Can you see the power of your belief system? Can you see how living abundantly is an inside job? Your path to freedom and bliss is directly linked to the way you think and what you choose to believe. It is time to let go of the beliefs that blocks your access to "more"; more love, more joy, more adventure, more divine connections, more time, more flexibility, more physical health, more finances, more peace, more celebrations and more freedom.

It is reflection time. Take an inventory of your experiences to identify what may be blocking your path. Connect with your personal why. Who else will benefit from you living abundantly besides you?

_____

_____

Complete the following sentences.

I look forward to enjoying more _____

An abundance of _____ will give me the freedom to ___

_____

I am open to and willing to receive _____

Write thoughts of lack that you've heard in your lifetime in the Lack Consciousness column. Think about empowering and life affirming thoughts. Write them in the Abundance and Prosperity column.

Lack Consciousness	Abundance & Prosperity

Radical ways to live abundantly

- Make peace with what you have by expressing gratitude for having it. This includes your physical, spiritual and emotional health.
- Release any shame, guilt or judgment associated with abundance.
- Pay close attention to your body and what it is telling you.
- Know your numbers. Consistently track your spending.
- Create a personal joy account. Deposit funds to do things that bring you joy.
- Honor truth and integrity in everything you do.
- Celebrate even the smallest shifts towards growth.

Today I celebrate.....

_____

_____

_____

(Aha moments) Today I discovered....

_____

_____

_____

_____

I felt great when......

_____

_____

_____

_____

_____

Radical Dreams

Every great dream begins with a dreamer. Always remember, you have within you the strength, the patience, and the passion to reach for the stars to change the world.
Harriet Tubman

Let's establish what it is that you really want. Forget about making it sound pretty or impressive. Think about what you really want without concern for how others may perceive it. What other people think about you is none of your business. It is a waste of your time and energy. It may also take you off your path. You don't want that to happen do you?

I believe that you can create the life you want. You can live boldly. You can love courageously. It all starts with you daring to confidently speak what you want. Say it loud. Say it proud. Say it without apologizing for wanting it. You don't owe anyone an explanation for wanting a fabulous life. You do owe it to yourself to get up, get out, go forth and create it. I did not say wait for it to come to you. I said create it. Remember that you co-create the life you live. Opportunities to have more and be more will show up in your life at the moment you begin to believe that you want wants you.

Living boldly is simply taking steps that move you closer to your dreams even when it scares you. Take steps that move you closer even when your friends and family don't understand it. That looks and feels different for everyone. Your fabulous life is defined by you. You don't have to live in the proverbial box. You can create your own box. Maybe for you the box itself doesn't exist. For you it may be an ocean where there is fluid movement. Whatever, it is know that God has a purpose and vision for your life. You may see or hear of other people doing what you want to do. So what? Your vision may appear to be similar to someone else's but it is still uniquely yours. You are not a clone of anyone. You are you. Don't let that stand in your way. There are people out there waiting specifically for you to show up on their path. You are destined to serve them. It is time to get radical in your dreams. Stand in your own brilliance. Add your personal touch to it and keep it moving.

Loving courageously is simply saying 'Yes' to things that lead to peace, joy and fulfillment. Say 'Yes' to behaviors, things and experiences that add value to your life. We say 'Yes' to many things. Unfortunately, some of those things, habits and people lead to stress, disappointment and unrest.
I said that I like to see others happy, and I do. Are you choosing to participate in support of others to add value to their lives? There

is distinct difference between doing what aligns with your current reality and doing something to blend in. Are you agreeing to participate out of obligation or fear of what others may think of you? Sometimes, we are so concerned with people pleasing that we forget that we are worthy of being pleased as well. It can be as simple as this.

Career/Profession
- Consistently taking work related calls after work hours.
- Agreeing to extra task because you want your boss to see you as indispensable.
- Choosing a career path because that's what your parents wanted you to do
- Remaining at a place of employment because someone told you that it would be crazy for you to seek employment elsewhere

Financial
- Hosting and paying for a baby shower or bridal shower when it's not in your spending plan
- Buying gifts with funds allocated for bills

Family/Friends
- Rescuing family from every situation they choose to create for themselves
- Making excuses for choices of family/friends
- Participating in activities you no longer enjoy

Dating Relationships
- Settling for less than your best for the sake of saying you're in a relationship
- Participating in sexual activities you don't enjoy to please your partner

Religion/Spirituality

- Committing to various ministries to look good and prove your love for God to members
- Saying that you're blessed and highly favored when you don't feel blessed or favored

There is a cost to agreeing to something simply to please someone else. If you are only doing it to please someone else then you are leaving an equally important person out of the equation. That person is you. Can you relate to any of this? In order to fully love courageously means to have the courage to love YOU first. Pour into you first and give from your overflow.

Learning to receive is equally important. Remain open to receiving help and support from others. You don't always have to be the pitcher doing the pouring. Sometimes you can be the cup and let someone else pour into you. It is totally okay to receive. Are you open and willing to receive love, joy and wealth?

This isn't about tangible things you want to have in your life. It is deeper than that. Get clear about your why? Why do you want what you want? This is really about what those things represent for you. I want multiple six figures available in my bank accounts to play with if I choose to. That is separate from funds for my personal living expenses. Why do I want it? It's not because I want to be wealthy for the sake of wealth. I want to have an abundance of resources available to serve others. One resource happens to be money. Access to cash gives me time freedom. My mother needs care. This time freedom will give me the flexibility to spend quality time with my mother without concerns about money or using personal leave from a job.

I want to create generational wealth for my grandchildren and my grandchildren's grandchildren. I want to be a living example of what is available when you step into your purpose. I want to be able to manage financial emergencies without using funds allocated for food, shelter and clothing for my family. If I use bill money to pay for home repairs, car repairs, vacations and other miscellaneous events, then I am living above my means.

I want my business to move from solopreneur to a thriving enterprise. Why do I want that? I want to expand my business to contribute to the employment and advancement of others. The personal benefit for me is that my business will run in my absence.

I want a beautifully decorated home that exudes peace and some excitement. Is this because I want a beautifully decorated home for to brag or show off? Absolutely not! It is because I want to feel at peace in my home. I want to walk in pleased with the environment in which I live. I work from home. I require a space that ignites the fire within me. It is imperative that I work in an environment that stimulates my creative juices. I need to be able to create content and products that serve the masses. Why do I want to serve the masses? I want to serve the masses because I saw that in the vision God gave me. My gifts were meant to be shared and experienced not trapped in my head stuck in idea form. What I know for sure is that I am not alone in this. Your gifts were meant to be shared as well.

I want to travel connecting with women all over the globe. Why do I want it? Women like you are phenomenal beings. I am moved to tears when I see women standing fully in their power. I absolutely enjoy contributing to breakthroughs, transformation and aha moments. Knowing that changing a woman's life literally changes the world really fills my love cup to overflow.

Let's get back to you. It is time to get radical with your heart's desires. Forget about perfection. Forget about playing safe. Forget about playing small. Answer the following questions to identify your desired destination. What lights up your world? What pulls at your heartstrings? What are the things that get you excited even when it's in your imagination? What do you want? If you could have anything you want, what would that be?

_____

_____

_____

What makes this important to you?

_____

_____

_____

What impact will it have on your life personally? What are the benefits of achieving these things?

_____

_____

_____

What impact will it have on your life professionally?

_____

_____

_____

How will your family's life change as a result of you creating the life you want?

_____

_____

Who will it help? How will others be blessed as a result of you stepping into your destiny?

_____

_____

_____

What life changes would you like to see happen within the next 21 days?

_____

_____

_____

What's stopping you? What are your perceived obstacles? (not enough money, support, time, etc.)

_____

_____

_____

Your obstacles are only as real as you believe they are. It may be tied to an old story that you've been telling yourself. It is time to divorce your old story. Create your new breathtaking story. Obstacles only have the power that we give them. Explore. Brainstorm. How can you move past, move around or walk through your perceived obstacles?

_____

_____

_____

When and if you find that you are in a place where it is difficult to see past where you are, STOP. Ask these questions.
What am I afraid of experiencing?

_____

_____

_____

What's the worst thing that could happen?

_____

_____

Sometimes the thing we're afraid is only real in our heads. Speak life into your vision. Shift your language to the place of possibility.

> *"The distance between you and everything you want*
> *is your language." Lisa Nichols*

What could possibly be available to me if the thing I'm most afraid of never happens? _____When your destiny appears to look similar to an unhealthy or painful place you've been before, STOP. It is easy to default into old habits because of its familiarity. Remind yourself that your past is not the sum total of who you are. Let your history be your guide. You have the data. You know where that path leads. Use the lessons of your past to propel you into a brighter future.

When you feel stuck in a situation, then you aren't reaching far enough. That's an indication that you are afraid to press forward. That means you've come to the line where familiarity and change intersect. The only way to know what lies ahead is to step forward.

Keep it simple. It takes one step to get started.

A journey begins with a single step. You don't have to do it perfectly. Take imperfect action. What one action will take me closer to my
desired destination?

_____ _____

Choose to make the necessary shift to cross the line of perceived
comfort to be your best self. I refer to it as perceived comfort because it is not really comfortable. If you were so comfortable where
you are, you wouldn't be complaining or secretly wishing for
something different. You would be content. We don't have a desire
to leave what feels good. I feel good and comfortable snuggled next
to my husband. I choose to venture out to fulfill my purpose for the
day. I have a clear understanding that I have a comfortable place
to enjoy at the end of my day. Do you see the difference? Comfort
is something you enjoy and get some sense of fulfillment. You can
lose track of time in this space. Discomfort is uneasy, unsettling,
and sometimes painful. It is something you want to escape.

Familiarity is what you have an association with. You've seen it
or experienced it before. It isn't as frightening because you know
what to expect. Remaining in a place of familiarity is beneficial as
you master the skills and lessons available to you. There comes a
time for you to graduate. It is time to grow. You do that by choosing
change over familiarity. Take the risk. What have you got to lose?
You have nothing to lose, but there is something to gain. What is
that something for you? Think of the possibilities ahead. How will
your life change as a result of pressing forward? The very thing you
may feel afraid of losing is possibly the main thing you need to release. You can always go back if you so choose. I don't recommend
it, but it is your choice.

Challenge yourself a bit more. What three steps are you willing to take to bring these goals into manifestation?

1. _____

2. _____

3. _____

Rate your beliefs on a scale of 1-10 (with 10 being the highest). How much do you believe that what you want will manifest in your life? Dig deeper if you did not rate your level of belief at an 8 or higher. What is limiting your belief? What will it take for you to believe it?

_____

_____

Radical ways to connect with your vision and dreams

- Seek God's guidance on your decisions and your direction
- Remain connected to your why
- Speak life into your vision by speaking what you want not what you don't want.
- Identify someone to hold you accountable
- Forget perfection. Take imperfect action steps
- Know that what you want wants you
- Align with like-minded people

Today I celebrate.....

_____

_____

_____

Today I discovered....

_____

_____

_____

_____

I felt great when......

_____

_____

_____

_____

_____

Nurtured Relationships

Everything is relationship. You have a relationship with friends, family, colleagues, food, God, money, your body, your environment and a relationship with yourself.

Every relationship is unique. We have different boundaries within every relationship. You may allow certain behaviors with one sibling, but not with another. You even have a different relationship with who you have become from who you were in your past. Each relationship holds value for you in some way.

One of the key things to consider as you think about your relationship is connection. How to do you fit or bond with a particular person, group or thing?

Let's look at food as an example. Ice cream is one of my favorite foods. I discovered that my love for ice cream has absolutely nothing to do with the way it tastes. My relationship with ice cream is associated with a memory. Ice cream was the snack I often ate before going to bed as a child. It is joyful childhood memory. I feel good when I eat ice cream. Do you see how that works?

Now let's take some time to explore your connection in the different areas of your life. Think about ways to nurture your existing relationships as you go through these questions. Take an inventory of your relationships. Let's start with you. Pay close attention to what happens to your body as you respond to each of these.

Personal Reflection:
What does a healthy relationship look like or feel like to you?

_____

_____

What helps you to consistently show up energetic and enthusiastic about each day?

_____

_____

When was the last time you felt valued? _____

_____

Describe what happened and who was involved. _____

_____

_____

How do you demonstrate acts of love and respect within each relationship?

_____

_____

Food: What is your favorite food?

_____

_____

What food or beverage do you crave when you need comfort?

_____

_____

What celebratory activities do you engage in that involves food/
beverages?

_____

_____

Do you prefer to eat alone or with company?

_____

_____

Why/Why not?

_____

_____

Family: Keep in mind that family does not have to be blood rela-
tives. Consider those you identify as family. In what ways does your
relationship with them support you in acquiring more joy, peace
and freedom?

_____

_____

Social Organizations: What groups or organizations do you belong to? Why did you join or get involved? What do you need to stay connected to your personal "why" that connects you to specific people, groups or organizations?

_____

_____

Professional Relationships: How would you describe your professional relationship? Write the name of 3 people that you work with on a consistent basis.

Other business entities: Name 3 places you spend money on a regular basis i.e... cable service, cell phone carrier, cleaners.etc. What restaurants, hair salons, nail salons, stores, do you frequent?

_____

_____

How do you feel when you go to these places?

_____

Do you effortlessly spend money with them or do you feel resistance when it's time to pay?

_____

_____

What keeps you coming back? What keeps you in these relationships?

_____

_____

Think about what's most important to you in business. Is it the customer service, rewards, your relationship with the staff, close to home, cost or something else?

_____

_____

Review your responses. Are there any relationships that you need to release? If so, how will you manage it? Who will support you? Which relationships would you like to make new agreements with and nurture? All of these questions are important because they align with your values and how you currently see yourself.

"Love is not something we give or get; it is something that we nurture and grow, a connection that can only be cultivated between two people when it exists within each one of them – we can only love others as much as we love ourselves." Brene Brown

Radical ways to nurture your relationships

- Spend quality with people you care about
- Give what you feel you are missing in your life. If you want more respect, give respect; more support, be supportive, to feel valued, make others feel valued, to be heard then actively listen to others
- Engage in open and honest dialogue
- Respect the perspective of others
- Seek clarity. Never assume that you know what others want from you or that they know what you want or need from them.
- Dare to have the difficult conversation. Embrace diversity

Energy Awareness

"Energy flows where your attention goes." Unknown

"What gets your attention gets you." Unknown

This pendulum can flow in the direction of expansion or constriction. I had an incredible week. I am making progress on this book you're reading right now. That brings me tremendous joy.

I started writing this book 2 years ago. What started as a fun project that felt like a wonderful gift to share with the world suddenly began to feel much like a burden. It felt a great deal of pressure to say the right thing to the right audience. My creative flow was difficult to access.

Go ahead and call me melodramatic if you want. I don't care. Writing anything felt like struggle to me. I mean anything; articles, emails, curriculum for coaching programs, social media post and even my own personal journal.

Here's what happened. You see I started in the space of gratitude. I was clear that this whole concept was not me but coming through me. I was thrilled to be a conduit of information. I was off to a great start. The thought of being of service to women I may never have the opportunity to meet in person was exciting. Then this toxic chick I used to hang out with invited herself to my party. You've got it! My ego got involved. She reared her ugly head and said, whoa. Wait a minute. Who are these women you may never meet? If you don't know them, how can you possibly be of service to them? Really Melanie?!! You don't know what they want. You don't know what they need. Who do you think you are?

BOOM! Talk about letting the air out of my balloon. What a dream killer! My alive-o-meter dropped from a strong ten to negative twenty. I believed my inner critic. I absorbed her negative energy. I allowed her to suck the life out of me I released all power and authority to her.. I began to shrink and become metaphorically invisible.

"Positive or negative energy is exchanged like a fair trade, the more you give, the more you receive." ~ Master Jin Kwon

In the midst of all of that, I experienced some highs but more lows. I continued to pray, listen to motivational messages, listen to pod-cast, read inspirational books and attend webinars. I invested in myself. I enrolled in coaching programs with coaches that I admire. I am pleased to report that today there is a shift in the atmosphere.

The information I absorbed and the people aligned myself with were blessings. I had major aha moments and breakthroughs, especially within the past week alone. Today, I am living in the energy of expansion and abundance. It feels awesome!

My perspective shifted through my own journey of self-discovery. I was reading Money: A Love Story: Untangle Your Financial Woes and Create the Life You Really Want by Kate Northrup. Let me tell you. That book had me on a well-oiled emotional roller coaster. Seriously, it took me for a ride that shook things up inside, pushed some out, reorganized others and temporarily disrupted my being. First of all, she and I have aligned values and beliefs. Secondly, parts of her book are similar to mine. I never heard of her before last week yet it was like she knew me, personally. We have similar habits and complimentary sabotaging behaviors. That totally stopped me in my tracks.

(She's back. Insert ego here.)I began to question whether or not I should continue writing. There was a conversation in my head that went something like this: Didn't Myles Monroe say something like God gives more than one person similar ideas. Only a few of us are going to act on it any way. Don't you tell your clients that we each get the opportunity to add our own personal touch to the journey? So why should I let her book stop mine? We don't have the same audience any way, right? But wait! None of this is about me. I am simply the vessel. This isn't about Kate. This is about me walking in obedience.

I continued to read further and connected with her prayer. I don't know where you are in the world right now, but I am forever grateful to you for writing your book. Everything shifted in the direction of expansion from there. I borrowed some of her words and added a few of my own. This is the Melanie remix.

God remove my ego from this space. Grant me the wisdom to share what others need to hear right now to come through as I type. I see myself as a receiver of what needs to be said and a translator to say it in a way that others may hear. God let your love shine through my translation. May your love expand within me. May the readers open their hearts, minds and souls to receive your love. May the world be filled with expansion of love and freedom as a result of it. It is an amazing honor to be a vessel and conduit of information transformation and healing. Let your will be done.

In this moment I live from a place of expansion and abundance. I released any and all attachments to what happens next. I am writing from my heart space not my head space. That energizes me. I feel so amazing that I wanted to share. I called by brother Bruce, my sister Karen and a few others. Guess what happened. Something in them expanded as well. I was excited to the point of silly. My husband and I were dancing and singing off key in the kitchen. Thankfully there are no hidden cameras in our home, because we were a hot mess and loving every minute of it.

I said all of that to remind you that what gets your attention gets you. I felt constricted when I focused on my inner critic. My ego had all of my power. Ego doesn't like to fail or look bad. She will keep you stuck. Shifting the focus from me, Melanie to God, my creator expanded my access to joy. I am free to lead from my heart not from external forces like the opinions of others. Make sense? Back to you, my sister, how will you choose where to direct your energy?

God in his infinite wisdom gave us bodies that speak to us. Listen to your body. It gives you clues as to what's happening within you and around you. Think about the activities that cause your body to tighten. In what areas of your life to you feel a high level of resistance? I'm sure you've heard, what you resist persists. Well that is absolutely true. What we resist expands and we experience that in which we resist.

Surround yourself with things that inspire you. What are the things that lead to the feeling or energy of abundance? Keep in mind that it is not the actual thing or item. It is what that represents for you. I enjoy hotels. I feel expansive and abundant when I enter a hotel lobby that exudes luxury and ambiance.

Spending time near water centers me. I enjoy watching the ripples in the waves with no idea of where it begins or ends. The lake or ocean is so expansive that I appear to be infinite. It's definitely too far for my eyes to send. That stirs something up inside of me. Some days I feel calm and relaxed. Other times I feel excitement, enthusiastic and ambitious. On those days I want to walk for miles by the lake, skip or even jump. I feel the same way about waterfalls. For me it models the flow of life. It has a steady rhythm and pace. It is connected to its own movement with a sense of certainty, assurance and purpose. I love that it's all water yet the waterfall doesn't try to be a lake. The lake doesn't try to be an ocean. That to me is energy of peace.

What energizes you? When do you feel most alive? I feel alive when I'm speaking to women about things I'm passionate about. I feel alive when I go to the schools and talk to young people. I feel energetic and alive when I hear my mother laugh. I feel ecstatic when my husband and I sing and dance at home. These activities can take my alive-o-meter from 1 to 10 in a matter of seconds.

Think about a time when you felt at your best. What happened that led you to feeling your absolute best? With whom did you share that moment? Did they celebrate you? How did you feel about being celebrated in that way? How did you celebrate? How long did this feeling last?
Think about the 5 people you listed in the relationship exercise in chapter 4. Who are the people who energize you? Who makes you laugh?

When do you feel at ease? When do you feel safe and/or secure? It is subjective. It is different for everyone. I like to fill my gas tank when it is half full. I feel at ease when I have gas in my car. I feel vulnerable whenever I am riding in a car on empty or even close to empty. From my perspective it creates more risk. It compromises my sense of security. It creates an opportunity to find myself stranded. Becoming a damsel in distress is not on my vison board. It gets cold in Chicago. I want to know that I can keep the car running to stay warm if there are any unexpected traffic delays or other unforeseen incidents that are beyond my control. Traffic is one of those thing in which I have no control But I can control the amount of gas in my tank. For me it is just that simple.

That one example is an energy leak. My energy shifted just writing about it. Let me tell you about something else that is an energy leak for me, other people's drama. I can't speak for you but I swear there are people whom I love that I believe are addicted to drama.

Seriously?!! Is there a 12 step program for drama magnets? Let me tell you. They are by no means selfish with it either. The call friends and family to spread the drama. But it doesn't stop there. They share it with the world on social media.

"Some people create a storm then complain when it rains."
-Unknown

It's toxic energy that spreads like a virus when you don't manage it. I used to get upset. I used to let it shift my mood and rain on my parade. It bothered me that there was so much turmoil and chaos in their relationships. Then I learned the art of acceptance. I accept that this is their personal choice. I don't have to like it or agree with it. .However, I accept it. This is how I manage that now. I choose not to participate. I choose not to follow them on social media. I choose not to get upset when they are upset. I choose not to allow their mess to become my mess. And that my dear, is an act of self-love.

What are your energy leaks? Which activities or behavior leaves you feeling depleted?

_____

_____

Radical ways to be mindful of your energy

- Listen to you body. It gives you clues.
- Participate in activities that makes your heart dance
- Place things in your space that bring you joy
- Tune in to the energy around you, including conversations
- Remain mindful of your inner dialogue
- Use mantras to keep you focused on what you want
- Use photos or other visuals that remind you of how amazing you are

Today I celebrate.....

_____

_____

_____

Today I discovered....

_____

_____

_____

_____

I felt great when......

_____

_____

_____

_____

Radical Self-Love

Who or what is most important to you? I ask this question often during my seminars. The most common responses are God, family, career and finances. You may have answered in the same way. Who is missing from the list? If you answered me, you're absolutely correct! Too many of us, especially women forget to put ourselves on the list of important people. All too often we fail to see ourselves as the most important person.

That doesn't sit well with me. There is something terribly wrong with seeing a picture of your life and you are the missing image; totally absent from your own life. YOU are the most important person in your life! You cannot take care of anyone when you have nothing left to give. God breathed life into you to live and to live fully with purpose and intention. How can you honor that if you continue to devalue your existence? You are required to participate in your own life. God gave you free will. How you participate is totally up to you.

I dare you to choose love as the main theme of your life. God is love. Let love guide you. Your love for you is a huge part of that. You get to choose to recognize your existence as valuable and meaningful. Your family can't afford for you to ignore that your life matters. Choose you. Vote for you. How will you unapologetically say 'Yes" to loving you today? Is self-care or me-time listed anyway on your calendar?

Give this some serious thought. Continuing to ignore your needs will potentially cost you and those you love. Look at the big picture. This may hurt but I'm going to ask you the hard question. What will happen to your loved ones if you continue at this pace and something happens to you? That may be difficult to think about but a reality check is in order. Sometimes I feel like I'm fighting for the lives that some of you can't even see that you're losing.

Now I am going to shift the energy by asking it in the affirmative. How will taking care of you help your family?

_____

_____

In what ways will self-care help your cause?

_____

_____

How will self-care support your business? (if applicable)

_____

_____

I am not exempt. Reality checks are real for me too. Sometimes the life I am fighting for is my own. My life shifts to a space of lack when my thoughts and actions are out of alignment with God's will. Life may look like there is not enough during those times. That is when I may take my circumstances personal and feel like I am not enough. Therefore, I co-create more lack. You may have heard this before, but I am going to say it again. You are enough, regardless of your current situation. Know that you are enough. I was speaking to The Profit Accelerator, Allyson Byrd one day. I mentioned that I teach what I most need to learn. She told me that my next intensity of self-love is to show that my love is real for me. Whew! That hit me hard. It resonated because I needed to be reminded of that in that very moment.

I created a "Self-Love" t-shirt line. Marketing self-love is really interesting partially because many believe that they love themselves. I respectfully disagree. I would argue that many of your behaviors are not aligned with self-love at all. If you are not incorporating self-care in your daily routine, you are missing the mark.

So how do you define self- love? I encourage you to consistently take an honest inventory of our love walk. Do you purposely walk in love? Take a moment to reflect on the past 2 weeks. List 3 things that you did that represented self-care or self-love.

1. _____
2. _____
3. _____

Women are nurturers and givers. We will give until we've given ourselves away. At the root of your need to please, financial woes, unhealthy relationships are tied to the core of your love for yourself, your relationship with you. How can you position yourself to serve others including your family without neglecting the wholeness of you?

_____

_____

We talked about mind-body connection earlier. When we are not taking care of ourselves from a holistic perspective it will manifest physically in our bodies.

Value your life enough to cherish your body and treat it well. It's all inclusive, mind, body and soul.
Melanie Foote-Davis

Eat to Live

I love one of the lines in the animated movie Over the Hedge. This isn't verbatim but it's something like, animals eat to live and humans live to eat. Eat when you're hungry. Play close attention to when you're eating simply because the food is in front of you. Eat that which nourishes your body. I am more likely to eat healthy when I prepare my food ahead of time. I am more likely to eat food that makes me feel sluggish or sick when I wait until I'm starving. You will notice a difference in the way you feel when eat nourishing foods. Sadly eating on the go has become a way of living. I encourage you to take time to sit down to eat. Make it a habit to actually savor the flavor and enjoy your meals. Don't forget to hydrate..

"Watching their glory today doesn't tell you the struggle

of their yesterday"
Melanie Foote- Davis

Comparison Syndrome
It's one thing to acknowledge the success of another to celebrate their wins. It's another thing to ask why them and not you. I refer to this as the Comparison Syndrome. Be very careful. This can be a vicious and dangerous cycle.

- Comparison is a form of self-abuse
- Compete with you to grow into your next level
- Comparing breeds envy, resentment, self-loathing
- Counter-productive
- Takes you off your intended path. It's a distraction.
- It leads to self-destructive thoughts & behavior.
- It robs you of today's your joy.

Are you on social media watching what everyone else is doing? Be conscious of your intention. How do you choose who you follow? What keeps you peeking into the window of their virtual life? Do you follow them because you admire them, they make you laugh, inspire you to be your best or because you feel like kindred spirits? Are you celebrating them by liking and sharing their posts? Or are you angry because they're doing what you're not? Be honest. Be clear. What lessons can you learn from them?

The emotion associated with the success or failures of others is actually more about you than it is about them. Tune into it. What is it teaching you about who you are and what you want? How can you grow in this space?

Here's the thing. You are awesome and amazing too.
The biggest difference between you and that person is that they
took action and you didn't. They were consistent. You gave up.
They took action while you were still thinking about it. They dared
to try while you toyed with the idea.

Shift your perspective. They are not your competition. They are
your model. See them as an example of what's possible for you.
Thank them for paving the way. You can do it. Love yourself enough
to give it a try.

There is something else I would like for you to try.
Give yourself permission to receive compliments. Breathe it in. Say
thank you. Then stop talking. It's just that simple.

Give yourself permission to release the reigns a bit. What is your
belief system associated with asking for support?

_____

_____

How awesome would your life be it you willingly welcomed support?

Has this question ever secretly crossed your mind? "Hey! Can a
sister get some assistance?" Here's my answer. Yes. You absolutely
can. Here's the thing. Does anyone know that you need help? I bet I
can describe your favorite outfit. It has a wonder woman-like image that reads "I got this" The back of the outfit reads. "It's already
handled! I got that too." You wear it almost every day under what
we can see. Hopefully you've taken it off or at least considered now

that you've gotten this far in the book.

What's your story? In other words, what do you believe that are you gaining by continuing at this pace?

_____

_____

What are you possibly losing by continuing at this pace?

_____

_____

Who will it help?

_____

_____

Who will it possibly hurt?

_____

_____

What will you and your family possibly gain by making small changes?

_____

_____

Take an inventory of your current responsibilities. List 5 things on your Honey Do List.

1. _____

2. _____

3. _____

4. _____

5. _____

Everything is up for negotiation. You don't have to accept or say yes to everything that is presented to you. Choosing to accept responsibilities out of obligation may lead to resentment. Examine the list. Which tasks were perceived as things you had no choice about but you actually volunteered to do?

_____

_____

Create wins by making it work for you and them. Identify the negotiable and non-negotiable items on your list. Strongly consider renegotiating your agreement.

Which of these tasks do you enjoy and do well?

_____

There may be things that you know how to do, but you may not enjoy doing. Delegate the tasks that drain you. This will free up your energy to be more productive. Which tasks deplete your energy just by thinking about it?

_____

_____

Who do you know that is naturally skilled in this area? (Consider hiring someone to do it if necessary.)

_____

See the blessing in leveraging the gift and talents of others. Weigh the pros and cons of doing it yourself versus building a support team. How much of your time would be free to give back to nurturing your relationship with your family if you let some of these responsibilities go?

Radical ways to love you from a place of power

- Be the star of your self-love story
- Choose you on a daily basis
- Spend less than you earn
- Accept that you are perfectly imperfect and beautiful being
- Honor your temple by eating well, exercise and feeding your mind with inspiration and positivity
- Give yourself permission to slow down, take a break and ask for help
- Embrace support and recognized it as strength
- Accept compliments. Say thank you.
- Listen to podcasts or read things that inspire you
- Set clear boundaries.
- Renegotiate your agreements when needed
- Converse with positive people
- Practice saying this aloud. "Absolutely! I welcome your support." Awesome! I Appreciate Your Support"
- Acknowledge and embrace your gifts and talents
- Schedule regular Self-Love Days. Place personal time on your calendar to nurture your mind body and soul.

Today I celebrate.....

_____

_____

_____

Today I discovered....

_____

_____

_____

_____

I felt great when......

_____

_____

_____

_____

Unimaginable Love

The loving relationship that you've always dreamed of begins with your loving relationship with yourself. The love that only seems like a fantasy to some starts with fantasy-like romance within you.

Let me share a quick story. I was in love with a nice man. We shared a fascinating and perplexing non-committed relationship. For years we both dated whomever we wanted. Both of us had challenges with commitment. A part of me wanted to be in a committed relationship. A bigger part of me was totally terrified at the thought of being hurt and disappointed. I experienced waves of feeling unworthy and unwanted. Remember we are co-creators. I subconsciously protected my heart by attracting men who were just as afraid of commitment as I was.

I felt most powerful when I believed that I was in control. I determined when I would or wouldn't see him. I only agreed to hang out with him when I felt strong enough to accept the truth about what was going to happen. The reality was that it may be months before we hung out again.

We shared beautiful moments together during our trysts. Yes there was a physical attraction, but that wasn't what pulled me in. The connection for me was shared through quality conversations. We had aligned passions. We both found fulfillment by serving others. We shared a passion for young people. There was an unspoken knowing that it was safe to share my dreams, aspirations, fears and challenges without feeling judged. He had that in me as well. We were able to be vulnerable with each other with the exception of a long-term committed dating relationship. We risked telling each other the truth for the sake of helping the other dig deeper into our own personal growth.

One day, I realized that it was mysteriously magical yet dysfunc-tional. I was drawn to the idea of what he represented. Our time together represented acceptance, connection and passion for help-ing others find their voice. I was in love with the idea of having that type of connection within a romantic relationship. I accepted that he wasn't available to me full-time. I never tried to force him to be more that what he was willing to offer. He accepted that I needed to feel in control. I managed that by positioning when and where we would share these fleeting moments. But that's where the prob-lem lived. It lived in the pure fact that we were only comfortable with fleeting moments, not longevity.

I discovered that I wasn't as in control as I thought I was. As long as I was secretly hoping that one day he would want to be in a committed relationship with me, I was unknowingly giving my power away. My heart was held captive. How could I feel free to fully love another man when I was essentially reserving my love for the day that was never going to come? Or maybe it was, but I had some sense of clarity now. I was no longer willing to wait for the maybe one day we will...

You see I thought that I was experiencing freedom because I was calling the shots. Sure I occasionally dated other men with the expectation of them disappointing me thus giving me a reason to walk away and get back to my life. With the exception of one other guy, I was not open to give commitment a real chance.

I mastered art of being a single mother of an amazing daughter. Watching her grow from a sweet infant into a phenomenal woman was my greatest accomplishment. After all a part of my identity was centered around changing the perception and stereotype of being a black teenage mother. I chose to be alone most of the time instead of wasting time with men who were destined to disappoint me anyway.

Was that true freedom? Absolutely not! I was not free because I was guarding my heart. That also meant that I was avoiding risks, fun and adventure. I played it safe by hanging out with guys who were my platonic friends. They weren't going to disappoint me romantically because my expectations of them were to simply enjoy their company and their friendship, no more, no less. That was my fun. There was no need to guard my heart with them.

I called my special friend that I spoke of earlier on the day that I had life-changing aha moment. You know the day that I heard a voice say that I will never be totally free to love someone else until I release my attachment to the connection that I only shared with him. Not only was it unfair to me, but it was unfair to all of the men who were interested in dating me. They never had a fighting chance.

"Man in your heart is not necessarily the man in your dreams"
-unknown

I reached out to him. I began to share with him that I was freeing myself. I told him that I was releasing him to move on with his life. I was choosing to no longer hold my heart captive. I decided that I was going to spend time getting to know me a little better. He listened. He asked if we could talk in person. I was at peace with my decision to let go. I happily agreed to meet him at the park. We had an amazing time. We talked for hours. It was a beautiful sunny day. It was a day that I will never forget. Why? I will never forget the freedom that I felt that day. I will never forget the joy in knowing that I was taking a firm stand for me.

That was a beautiful step towards self-love. It wasn't about looking outside of me. It was about having peace within. That is true bliss. That is a feeling worth bottling up and serving by the gallon. I have no idea how to place a value on that because it is truly priceless. My heart smiles as I reminisce.

Let's fast forward to a few months later. Well I don't know the exact time frame. What I know for sure is that it was within a 3 month window. I was in no way even thinking about a romantic relationship. I was enjoying me in a new and exciting way.

I was in Las Vegas with my mother and my four sisters. My sisters and I went to Fatburger to grab a bite to eat. I was involved in a network marketing company at the time. My challenge was to introduce myself to anyone within 3 feet of me. I was feeling fearless, assertive and free. I saw this guy whom by the way, I was not attracted to. He was handsome but all I saw was a business opportunity. I introduced myself. He and I had a brief conversation about the business opportunity. I gave him my business card and we parted ways. I checked my voicemail later that evening. There was a message from the man from the burger place. I returned the call to schedule a meeting with him during my time in Las Vegas.

The most amazing thing happened. We talked for well over an hour. We scheduled an appointment. But it was everything but a business meeting. He asked me out on a date. I happily accepted. We had an amazing time. It was like hanging out with an old friend. We laughed, played games the arcade, listened to a band at one of the casinos and walked the strip. We enjoyed each other's company so much that afternoon. I had dinner plans with my mom and sisters. We agreed to see each other again later that same evening. So we actually had two dates on the same day. We hung out until 4:00am-ish the next morning. They say whatever happens in Vegas stays in Vegas. Sometimes we make exceptions. This was one of those times.

That handsome dude, Sean, whom I was not attracted to, is now my husband. We continue to date each other. We still enjoy each other's company. So what! I wasn't attracted to him the day I met him. He wasn't even my so called type. But guess what? What I thought was my type was absolutely not working for me. Sean whom I affectionately call my Sugarbear is totally my type now. I am beyond attracted to him. You want to know something else? I no longer feel unwanted or unlovable. I feel loved and wanted every day now. Life has thrown us some intense waves. We rode the waves together with love as our life jacket. Sean is supportive of me and my endeavors. He listens to me for hours on end; trust me I talk a lot. Lol. He makes me laugh. He reminds me to have fun.

I am a living, breathing star in my own romance novel. None of this would've been possible had I not honored and trusted the voice of wisdom on that glorious day. Being obedient to that voice led to making radical decisions about my dating relationship and essentially my life. I did not over-think it as I am known to do. I simply trusted the wisdom and took action. Each day I am continuing to have radical love within my marriage. Most importantly I am experiencing radical love for myself.

I get to experience unconditional love and romance with my husband. What was once unimaginable and far-fetched is now a part of my personal ever-expanding love story. However, this love wasn't available to me until I was open to first connect with what made sense for me on a soul level. Secondly I needed to remain open to receive the love. It was not easy for a woman who had mastered the art of guarding her heart. Sean was patient with me as I learned to receive his love. I promise you, I didn't make it easy for him. Honestly, I have days when I feel challenged by it. But Baby when I am in receiving mode, that loving feeling is absolutely delicious. (Side note: Sean and I tell one part of the story of how we met differently. Just to be clear, my version is how it happened. Lol!)

Radical ways to embrace unimaginable love
- Your love story begins within you (inside job)
- Trust your inner wisdom
- Become your own best friend
- Know your worth
- Listen to your body
- Enjoy the romance
- Relax and have fun
- Move out of desperation and into your destination
- You can't truly say yes to what you want until you say no to what you do not want.
- Be willing to go of what doesn't add value to your love story
- Revisit the story of how you met if you are beginning to feel disconnected in your existing relationship

Today I celebrate.....

_____

_____

_____

Today I discovered....

_____

_____

_____

_____

I felt great when......

_____

_____

_____

_____

Peace Be Still

Living a stress-free life calls for a few simple things. I may not seem simple we like to complicate things.

Listen to your body. It speaks to you in many ways. Trust your intuition. I like to think of it as God lovingly guiding my path with sweet whispers. Here's the thing. You may not hear clearly if you're too busy running around. You may not hear if your life is full of noise. Technology has its purpose but how much is too much? You are receiving messages all day. Are you able to hear the message that was specifically meant for you? It is imperative that you make time to be still and get centered.

The key to connecting with your source is to disconnect from external forces. Yes I am asking you to turn it off. Unplug it all. Disconnect from technology and connect with you and the one who guides you. Relax. I am not asking you to unplug forever. Start small. Schedule fifteen minutes a day without your phone, internet or television. You're not missing anything. Choosing to stay connected to external forces and energies may cause you to miss out on you and everything that is important to you. You can find it all there when you log back on.

Tune into what is present. Is your mind full or are you mindful? Mindfulness and being present to your now moments helps you experience life to the fullest.

> *"Wherever you are, be all there"*
> *JimElliot*

Earlier I asked about who was important to you. Family or friends may have been your response. If that is true for you then align your actions with your words. Multi-tasking and being fully present at the same time is not possible. Just because your body is physically present doesn't mean that you are emotionally present for the people you care about.

Others feel disconnected when you're not emotionally present. Deep down inside they want your presence not your presents. Being mindful is about being with whatever it is that you are doing. Put your phone down, look your children in the eye and actively listen to what they are sharing. Otherwise they may not come to you when they really need you because they may feel like they are bothering you. Connect with those riding in the car with you by engaging in quality conversation. Show your family that they matter through intentional connections. Watch your world shift.

Others way to be mindful and connect is by eating a meal without checking your cell phone. Eat slowly to savor the flavor. Read a great novel. Escape and fully immerse yourself into the story. Take a journey with the author. Connect with each part of your body as you bathe. The next time you ask someone how they are doing, actually listen to the answer.

Live in the present by noticing where you are. Connect with nature. Listen to the sounds around you. I like to lie on my back and watch clouds move and reshape. Get sunlight daily. It will energize you.

It is absolutely necessary for me to be intentional about creating quiet time. Taking time to be still and get centered keeps me grounded. I tend to notice patterns or cycles. Clutter shows up for me when I lose sight of my personal quiet time. It may be physical clutter or it may be mental clutter. For me they go hand in hand. My physical space begins to fill whenever my mind is full and fighting for clarity. My office begins to collect stacks of paper. My email inbox is full. Everything around begins to feel chaotic and disorganized. Some people thrive in organized clutter. I don't. It throws me completely off my game. I find no peace in that.

The way that I get back on track is by releasing the clutter. I am the first to admit that I don't nip it in the bud at the first sign of it. I tend to wait until I am emotionally charged and beginning to feel stuck. Hey! Don't judge me. I am perfectly imperfect, remember? At that point I begin to sort through. I keep what is here to serve me. I purge what I no longer has purpose and meaning. I get clear about what that is and what it represents for me.

What about you? Are you consistently organized or do you have a tendency to collect clutter like me? Remember I am speaking of physical and mental clutter. Are you holding on to anything from your past that is blocking your present and future? How will you embrace new possibilities when you're holding on to things and people that are taking up space in your life? Is it crowding your space with joy or is it keeping you stuck and unmovable?

"Forgiveness is an act of the will, and the will can function regardless of the temperature of the heart."
Corrie Ten Boom

Forgiveness is not an easy feet. However, it is necessary if freedom and peace of mind are experiences that you desire. One of the things that make it difficult to forgive is the belief that forgiving the person is letting them off the hook for their transgressions. Holding on to the pain or the story associated with it hurts you more than the person who did it. It is toxic to your body and your soul. Lack of forgiveness is like drinking poison and expecting the other person to die. It is sort of like letting someone rent space in your heart and the only person paying to stay there is you. You pay with your pain. Where is the joy and freedom in that? There is none. In order to make room for the peace you desire you must choose to evict the toxic tenants in your heart. You may believe that holding on to it or keeping it close is a way of protecting yourself from hurting you again. It is essentially keeping you from that freedom you are longing for. Make room for more of what you want in your life by releasing emotions that stand in its way.

Accept that it has already happened. Ruminating and repeatedly thinking about the details leads you back into that pain of your story. That keeps you stuck in that moment in time, the past. Living in your past prevents you from fully experiencing your present. It doesn't allow you to move forward and take new steps towards the future that you want. What can you do to move past this? I am not asking you to forget it. Remembering it has its way of protecting you. Holding on to it will control you. Choose to move past things you've experienced. Make the decision to take your power back by choosing to stand on your story, not in your story. Choose to not let that life event run your life. It is just that simple.

Worry is a cycle of inefficient thoughts whirling around a center of fear. Corrie Ten Boom

Worry does not empty tomorrow of its sorrow. It empties today of its strength. Corrie Ten Boom

Faith and worry can't hang out in the same space. Choose one. I vote for faith. It is the one that serves you best. Be anxious for nothing. Let tomorrow take care of itself.
Tomorrow is God's business, not yours.
Melanie Foote-Davis

Live in gratitude. Be grateful for the simplest things. Give thanks for that which has yet to manifest. Appreciate what is already working for your good. Be grateful for the achievement of others. They helped you to see what's possible for you. Don't hate. Congratulate.

Radical ways to live in peace and serenity
- Disconnect. Get centered. Be still.
- Pray, meditate, aroma therapy, laughter
- Release your mental and physical clutter. Keep what you absolutely love and will use. Re-gift what you are not using, will not use and no longer feel connected to
- Free up your space to have and experience the things that bring you joy
- Release old stories and old beliefs about your story
- Be perfectly imperfect and let go of perfection
- Live in gratitude
- Live in the present. Let tomorrow take care of itself

Today I celebrate.....

_____

_____

_____

Today I discovered....

_____

_____

_____

_____

I felt great when......

_____

_____

_____

_____

Own Your Power

The author of Playing Big, Tara Mohr said that her mentor once said "American women are liberated but not empowered." That resonated with me on a cellular level. I know and have worked with powerful women who are influential within their own circles and beyond. Yet, I notice a pattern of succeeding in one area of their lives and struggling in others. They are challenged with work-life balance and trying to have it all. They experience a consistence imbalance of abundance in one hand and deprivation in the other.

It is what I call the Olivia Pope syndrome. She is a power player in business. She owns that space. She naturally thrives in that lane. She confidently steps up in the heat of the moment, performs a mental assessment and unapologetically makes difficult decisions to diffuse the situation.

Her personal life is in contrast of her professional life. At home there is uncertainty, loneliness and uneasiness. The distance between the two spaces is huge. I know women who live from that space. It breaks my heart. Sometimes I feel like I am fighting for the life that women don't even know they're losing. There is no peace, no freedom and no bliss in that. Believing that you have to choose to live in a "this or that" world as opposed to experiencing "this and that" is costing you. How do you win by having power and influence with no one to share it with? Who wins when you feel forced to choose either your career or your family?

What are you saying, 'Yes" to? It is time to renegotiate life on your own terms. It is your time to stand on the right side of your Yes; the side that feeds your soul.

"Our courage has not caught up with our opportunity" Claire Zammit of Emerging Women

Renegotiate on your own terms. No more playing small. No more whispering from the corners of your life and hoping someone will hear you. It is time to find your voice and speak your truth for the sake of your own justice. Be loyal to your dreams and desires in spite of what others may think of you. But do so with nothing to prove, nothing to defend and nothing to protect. Do it with good intention and for the benefit of all. It will also serve you.

You get to decide what success means for you. You get to decide what abundance feels like for you. Do work or participate in activities that you deeply care about or feel connected to. Let go of saving face or feeding the ego. Feed your soul instead. Feed your soul and you feed the world.

Leverage life in a way that frees up space for more of what you want. You get to decide what that is for you. What does power mean to you?

_____

_____

Identify one person who you deem as powerful.

_____

What are his/her characteristics?

_____

_____

How do these characteristics align with your definition of power?

_____

_____

Are these qualities or skills that you also possess or possibly one you aspire to have? Yes or No (circle one)

Do they represent your own hidden talents? Yes or No (circle one)

Have you ever minimized your talents out of fear of stealing spot light from someone else? Yes or No (circle one)

Surrender your need to know all of the details before taking action. It is not your responsibility to know where your next step will lead. Know that there is power in a pause. Pause. Take a break. Connect with that sweet voice of wisdom. Trust it. Move from that place within you that pulls and tugs at your heart. Move with grace and ease without attachment to the outcome.

Avoid basing your decision on what you believe to be the expec-tation of others. Quite frankly, you don't know what they want unless you ask or they tell you. Make decisions that lead you to the desired result. Let's keep it real. You will encounter fear. Understand that fear is coming place that wants to protect you. Your ego doesn't want you to look bad or fail. Feel the fear and do it any way.

You must be willing to dive deeper into the gap between freedom and the opportunities you desire. When you are sitting in fear you will only see the obstacles and why it won't work. Fear is projected into a future of what you don't want. That is living in the land of lack. Shift your thought process to what you want instead. Choose to live in the land of possibility and abundance. Align your inner wisdom with your actions. Enjoy the journey.

Radical ways to stand in your power
- Own your brilliance
- Stand on the right side of your Yes
- Negotiate on your own terms
- Feel the fear and move forward in spite of it
- Remain loyal to your dreams
- Align your inner wisdom with your actions
- Take inspired action
- Stand in possibility
- Be visible. Take Risks.
- Live faith in action
- Embrace your now
- Surround yourself with someone wiser than you
- Keep and open-mind
- Continue to learn
- Invest in your personal and professional growth
- Practice humility and gratitude
- Celebrate along the way

Today I celebrate.....

_____

_____

_____

Today I discovered....

_____

_____

_____

I felt great when......

_____

_____

_____

_____

Honor Your Emotions

Feelings are an important part of lives. We can't get away from them because we are experiencing all the time. Unfortunately, we've been culturally conditioned to ignore our emotions. Imagine a world where social emotional learning was a priority. It would be kinda cool right? Many of us were not taught that it is ok to feel specific emotions like sadness, confusion or disappointment. Clearly, no one told us what to do with these things called emotions. Well that's not actually true. Some of us heard things like, *"Get over it." "Suck it up" "Deal with it. That's just the way it is."* But that's the problem. They forgot to tell us how to deal with it. I'm going to walk you through a simple process in a few.

I was overjoyed when I learned that Disney Pixar was releasing a movie that addressed feelings called Inside Out. I really wasn't interested in another princess movie teaching girls that finding her prince was her only path to happiness. Oops... I digressed into a quick rant. Ok. I'm done. Thank you for the release. I saw the movie with my husband. Then my friend Tiffany and I took a group of kids to see it. I was pleased to see that they gave each emotion a purpose. Sadness supports connection and empathy. Fear wants to keep you safe. Anger wants fairness and justice. Simple right? We went out for pizza afterwards and had a rich discussion about feelings. They embraced the opportunity to fully express themselves. We had a blast!

The process is as follows:

1. Accept that we all have emotions.
2. Accept that there is nothing wrong with you for feeling. It is actually the other way around. I would be seriously concerned if you don't have emotions.
3. Let go of self-judgment for having that specific emotion
4. Honor your emotion by acknowledging that it exists.
5. Fully experience the emotion.
6. Release it

Look at how this plays out in these scenarios.
Let's look at John and his ex-wife Tammy. They had a daughter, Jessica. John was upset with Tammy. He believed that she made decisions that were based on her own needs cleverly disguised as something in the best interest of their daughter. She enrolled Jessica in extra-curricular activities and expected John to pay for them. She moved quite frequently. According to her she moved for Jessica. John noticed a pattern. Tammy seemed to move closer to her job. John saw that as a convenience for her and not really about their daughter. Sometimes she relocated to towns that were

60-80 miles away, few times she actually moved out-of-state. The distance made it more challenging for John to be physically present for Jessica's activities. Therefore he missed special moments that he would've loved to share with his daughter.

It was important for John to identify his emotion and get to the root of what it represented for him. He discovered that he was angry and disappointed. Justifying the emotion isn't what's most important here. Remember that it is healthy to have and emotion. It is how you respond to that emotion that often leads to unhealthy consequences. This is about owning and fully experiencing your emotion.

Jessica has two active parents. According to John these decisions were made by one parent and one parent only. There was an absence of healthy co-parenting conversations to discuss what both parties believed would be in Jessica's best interest.
In this situation, John learned that he felt powerless and disrespected. He felt like he no longer had a voice or any power to effectively co-parent their daughter. We hear about absent fathers far too often. Here is a father who actually spends quality time with his child. Her mother possibly unconsciously continued to build a wedge between them. John and Tammy can now have a different conversation with this information. It removes the blame and desire to make one person right and the other person wrong from the conversation. Together they can explore options from the perspective of doing what's best for Jessica.

I encourage you to feel whatever it is that you're feeling it is important. Address whatever emotion you are experiencing. If you're angry feel angry if you frustrated feel frustrated if you're disappointed, be disappointed. There on no good and no bad emotions. I like to look at emotions as your body's way of letting you know that something needs your attention. So let's do that. Give the emotion your attention. Fully process it without judgment. Once you process it, let it go. Release it because none of this has anything to do with the other person. It has everything to do with you.

Experience your full range of emotions. Life happens. The world isn't perfect. We will sometimes experience pain, disappointment, anger, frustration and sadness. When you're angry be angry. When you're sad, feel sad. When you're happy, fully experience that as well.

In the book Expectation Hangover, Christine Hassler talks about spiritual bypass. That really resonated with me because I've been guilty of that myself. I wanted to skip that and find the bright side instead of fully experiencing my own pain or creating the space for others to experience theirs. I am an optimist. I don't enjoy seeing others unhappy. I used to believe that if I got someone to see their bright side, I then I can help to quickly move them out of their pain.

Process Coaching was where I felt most challenged during my coaching courses. I don't enjoy seeing others in pain. I discovered that I wanted to move them out of their darkness because I was personally uncomfortable with their pain. I wasn't fully serving them from that place. Unprocessed feelings will resurface somewhere else down the road. Triggers won't have as much power over you once you learn how to acknowledge them. I'm sure you can relate. Have you heard someone trying to console a person who was upset to the point of tears? You heard them say, "Aww. Don't cry. It's going to be alright." By all means cry until your heart is content. I always feel better after a good ugly snotty cry. Their intention was to relieve the pain.

Needless to say, I am conscious of that now. At times I fall short. I am very intentional about holding the space for my clients gets what they want and need when and if the situation presents itself. I ride the storm with them knowing their freedom is on the other side of their breakthrough.

During my depression, I discovered that I refused to acknowledge my anger or my grief. I believed that I was too blessed to be angry. I suppressed my anger associated with my mother's accident. I never slowed down to grieve the loss of my father. They resurfaced because they longed to be acknowledged. I didn't wallow in them. I acknowledged them. I fully embodied the experience. I didn't know one person had that many tears. They are classic examples of un-processed emotions.

That is what I've learned to do with other emotions as well. I acknowledge my disappointment with some of my personal deci-sions and when my loved ones make unhealthy choices. I accept it as their choice in which I have now control. I release it.

The process is the same with emotions that feel good as well. I talked about joy and happiness in my marriage earlier. I was in a happy relationship but often minimized it whenever I was talking to friends who were unhappy in the relationship or not in a rela-tionship at all. That wasn't fair to my husband or me. I was ulti-mately suffocating our love. That's just plain foolish.

Honor your agreements. I felt out of balance and out of alignment when I broke an agreement with my husband regarding finances. It was my idea that we create an agreement around how we spend money. We agreed to use our joint account for bills and joint expenses. We have had personal accounts for personal expenses. It wasn't a secret we will both aware that the other party has personal accounts. So that wasn't the problem.

Here's the problem. The agreement was that we would not speak spend more than a set dollar amount without having a discussion and talking it through with each other. There was an opportunity that I was totally interested in. I made the decision to move forward with the intention to tell my husband about it later. Later meaning later that evening when we talked because I was out of town.

The appropriate choice would have been for me to wait until I spoke with hubby. I'm sure you can guess what I did instead. I reached for my card and completed the transaction. I won't disclose the dollar amount but it was four digits. I know. I know. Don't judge me. I'm human and prone to occasionally use poor judgement.

Every part of my being shifted. My excitement faded fast. The whole thing was unsettling. It wasn't because of the dollar amount. It was unsettling because I was out of alignment. I had broken an agreement with my friend, my husband and my partner. And that was not a healthy choice for either of us. The impact of that could've have compromised the trust that we shared as well as the integrity of our relationship.

I am in no way proud of that. It was a huge lesson for me. It was necessary for me to acknowledge my shame and guilt associated with my choice. You can avoid this simply by remaining aware of what you say yes to and what makes this agreement important to you. Pause to consider the possible outcome. Be intentional with what your agreements.

The possible impacts of suffocating your emotions are:
Mental or physical clutter, debt, loss of appetite, insomnia, easily irritated, excessive eating, binge sleeping, television, drinking, smoking, shopping, social media, spending, sex, need cleaning, exercise, headaches, nausea, anxiety attack, working extra hours, filling time with empty and unfulfilling activities. Please give yourself permission to seek support if you are experiencing any of these.

Radical ways to honor your emotions

- Journaling is a great tool to clear your mind.
- Acknowledge your feelings
- Feel without self-judgement
- Seek support when needed
- Process your feelings then release them
- Move your body to support the process. Sometimes a brisk walk helps to make sense of what you're feeling.
- Don't take anything personal. There is a lesson and a blessing in it

Today I celebrate.....

_____

_____

_____

Today I discovered....

_____

_____

_____

I felt great when......

_____

_____

_____

_____

Get Radical! Live Out Loud

I am so excited that you made it this far. Let's be silly. Play with me for a moment. Let's take a mental escape. Imagine your life painted in vibrant colors. Make your life like a skittle fanatic. Taste the rainbow by living in full color. Which colors help you feel powerful, beautiful and unstoppable? Live in colors that connect with the essence of who you are. Maybe you prefer soft pastels with an occasional pop of colors. You may feel more connected to warm earthy tones. Or you may love rocking black and white or something else. Which colors give you life and make you feel fun, playful and energetic inside and out? What are you doing in this magnificent piece of art you just created? I hope that whatever you were doing help you feel vibrant and exhilarated. That was fun right?! I enjoyed imagining what you created. I had flashes of beautiful women all over the world feeling happy and free. That made me feel yummy inside.

Speaking of color, I personally avoid color concepts that box me in.

Let me explain. I am a woman who thinks that pink is a pretty color. However, pink does not make me feel more feminine. I don't feel connected to pink in that way. It does nothing for me. Have I ever owned outfits or items in various shades of pink? Absolutely, but it is more about the whole outfit itself not the color pink alone. I never had nor have I ever had a desire to have a pink bedroom or a pink bike. To be perfectly honest I am irritated at the mere thought that all little girls absolutely must love like pink or purple. Why? I don't like it because I have an aversion to stereotypes. I don't like it because it places little girls in a box that she may or may not want to be a part of. I don't like it because it takes her voice away. I don't like it because it is not empowering.

I am not saying that little girls should not like pink and purple, many of them do. Pink or purple may be even be your favorite color. That is perfectly fine. There is nothing wrong with choosing pink or purple as your favorite color. What I am saying is that a girl who loves black, red, blue, green or a combination on the color wheel has the right to feel confident and empowered with what feels right for her. This isn't about favorite colors at all. The operative theme here is choice. This is about being empowered to choose even when it is not popular.

You can replace favorite color with other stereotypes or assumptions ie....career paths, job vs entrepreneurship, stay-at-home moms, dress vs pants, home based business, slim vs full figured, motherhood vs no kids, married vs single, cost vs value. At the end of the day, I will stand on the side that honors an individual's right to the healthiest choice for her.

One more thing before I move on from that is this. I stand for love. I stand for kindness. I stand for peace. I stand for empowerment. I stand for freedom. Using the color pink as an example may seem insignificant. I promise that it is not. I work in the schools. I see cruel comments on social media. I work with women and girls to find their voice and stand in their own power. All too often some-one is bullied or sexually harassed because they are different and don't fit neatly into a societal-norm box. It breaks my heart to know that families are torn apart, communities are devastated, young people are ostracized, suicidal and even dying because of a lack of acceptance and adherence to a box. Many of them are work-ing incredibly hard to accommodate someone else's expectation of them, quite often it is parents, family or peers. A belief system that has no tolerance for a person to play or color outside of the lines of these boxes causes emotional and sometimes physical harm. Some of you are afraid to seek professional support because of a stereo-type. For example, black people don't go to therapy. Bold face lie! I am black. I have hired therapist and coaches. I am not ashamed of that. Why would I? I am actually proud of it. It is one of the ways that I love and care for my well-being. This lack of acceptance is costing us far too many lives. That is not ok with me. It is unloving and unkind. It is about ego and power than it is about love, care and support.

This is not about Melanie feeling irritated. This is about an injus-tice of simple human rights. One of those rights is to feel physically, emotionally and spiritually safe. There is an energy leak when you strip a person of their dignity and power even in the tiniest ways. A part of my soul feels like it's dying when I feel confined or power-less. Consider times when you may have felt disempowered in your personal and professional life. . These terms are subjective. It's different for everyone. Let me share a few examples.

- Feeling stuck at a job you don't like
- Feeling like your ideas don't matter in personal or business relationships
- Feeling invisible or small in the presence of others
- Feeling like no one asked or considers you before making decisions
- Not feeling valued or significant
- Feeling like you have to blend in and follow what's socially acceptable
- Feeling like you don't belong or fit in
- You were berated or observed a manager a colleague in front of peers and didn't speak up for fear of losing your jobYou're in an abusive relationship but don't know how to leave safely
- Feeling like you can't leave an unhealthy relationship because of finances and/or children

These things can hugely impact your physical health and well-being. It may show up in a number of ways; high blood pressure, anxiety, depression, loss of appetite, insomnia, digestive issues, challenges with your reproductive system, headaches to name a few. Pharmaceutical companies are generating massive income because of it. (Full disclosure: I am not a medical professional. I believe prescription medications have its purpose just like anything else. I just don't believe it is the only solution to health challenges.)

I experienced depression a few years ago. Naturally my doctor wanted to prescribe prescription drugs. I refused to leave the office with the prescription. Let me tell you why. I had three main goals.

1. I wanted to get well and be healed.
2. I wanted to learn what caused this condition.
3. I wanted to get my life back.

The medication was not going to lead me to any of my goals. Did I want to feel better? Of course, I did. But I wanted to be healed even more. Helping me feel better temporarily was not getting me what I wanted, which was to be well. I wanted to get to the root cause of my depression. I did that by seeing a therapist and doing my inner work. It affected my ability to work and created financial challenges. My poor husband didn't know what he was going to come home to during that time. I may have been depressed but one thing was clear to me. I wanted to be healed and I was going to do on my terms. So I made a radical decision to fight for my life and my sanity. Baby, it was no cake walk. But I conquered it!

I value my health. I am fully aware that I have options I exercise my power to choose prevention and natural healing options without harmful side effects. I used pharmaceuticals as an example. Choose what is best for you in all areas of your life. My only request is that you take an honest look at the way you choose. Are your choices leading you to a healthier life? Or do you choose by default based on what you're used to or what will give you temporary relief for an ongoing challenge? Let me say it this way. If your life cycle keeps leading you the same place then it's time to choose something radically different.

It is quite hilarious to me that I am talking about being radical like it's a new word. Clearly it is not. The word radical was placed in my spirit. I was drawn to it for some reason. Now it seems to keep showing up wherever I am these days. It pops off the pages of what I read, including a recent devotion. I know that it is God telling me something. It is a clear reminder for me to graduate. That requires taking steps that may feel risky. It requires a disruption of comfort zones, even my own. The truth is I've been playing it too safe. It is time for some radical shifts. New beginnings are on the horizon. Some may be for me, some against me and some may decide later. That's the quite common in the land of growth.

This reminds me of a "get radical moment" from my past. It is one of my "go to" stories to tell because I found so much freedom as a result of it. What I know for sure is that we are not all wired the same. What works for me may not be a good fit for you. I am simply not cut out to have a traditional job long term. It doesn't vibe with my destiny. I have been blessed with opportunities to work in a variety of settings. Each of them prepared me for the next phase of my journey. I usually thrive at my jobs because I choose work that is purposeful and fulfilling to me. Well.... I thrive until my body tells me that something needs my attention. I typically listen to my body. I've noticed a consistent rhythm of signals that usually mean at least one of three things: a situation needs to be addressed and it's time to have a difficult conversation, company behaviors and values are out of alignment with mine or it is time to graduate and move on. I know something is going on when

- I lose enthusiasm about going into the place of business
- I begin to feel disconnected to the job or the atmosphere
- My body consistently tightens when I am performing certain

tasks
- I become easily irritated by things or people that didn't bother me before
- I begin to feel trapped, boxed in and confined
- The main reason I show up is for the paycheck
- My creativity is stifled
- My mood changes in the evening before work as I prepare for the next day
- I look forward to the end of a work day, holidays and off days
- I feel like there is so much more for me than this
- When my work begins to compromise my personal goals and aspirations

I was working at a major corporation. I was no longer feeling a sense of fulfillment. All of the signs listed were present. I knew that my season was coming to an end. I wanted to work towards building my coaching practice. But honestly, I had no strategic plan in place. Therefore the only thing keeping me there was feeling like "I had to" stay for the paycheck.

I heard a voice one evening while sitting at my computer writing content for my website. It wasn't loud. It was more like a whisper. But it was a firm authoritative whisper. I simply heard one word. "Resign" No. It didn't seem logical especially with no clear exit strategy, but I know what I heard. Most importantly, I know what I felt and believed with certainty. The message was very clear. My season was up. It was time to grow, time to graduate. When you grow out of your clothes it's uncomfortable to wear your old size. And you surely don't stay in high school when you receive your high school diploma do you? Graduation leads to the next level. It's funny how life can feel so free when you take inspired action.

I had no clue about my next steps. This was truly an act of faith. I had a conversation with the hubby. Although hesitant, he supported my decision to be obedient. I followed the voice of wisdom and resigned. My body relaxed just from typing the resignation. Handing that envelope to my manager was such a thrill. I think I floated out of the office that day. Working there had become the box and I wanted to break free. I walked down Chicago's Magnificent Mile feeling like the lyrics from Mary Tyler Moore show. "You're gonna make it after all!" All I needed was a hat to toss in the air. (That song probably means nothing to those of you born after 1970. Lol)

I knew that it was a security risk for me to continue to work the remaining 2 weeks which meant they asked for my keys and paid me for the 2 weeks. I had 2 weeks to create a strategy. Then the most amazing thing happened. Within a few days I received a phone call that led to a coaching contract. The contract was paying me more than the job was. Whoooohooo! How awesome is that?!!!! I didn't know my next step, but God know. (Warning: I do not endorse leaving your job without a plan unless you are clear that it is your divine next step.)

It's your turn! What does all of this mean for you? Are you longing to be released from your box? Is this your season to get radical and do what appears to be unreasonable? Maybe it's time for you to pursue or finish that degree you want. Maybe it's time to ask for that raise, the promotion you want or apply for a new place of employment. Or maybe for you it means empowering your adult-age children to become adults. Ouch. That one may sting a little but it can lead to less stress and a healthier life for all parties involved. Maybe it's time for you to relocate to a new city, or swallow your pride and get a roommate to help you achieve a financial goal. What about enrolling in that class or hobby that you've always wanted to try? Oh wait. I got one. Maybe you can use vacation days to take an actual vacation. Now that sounds like fun. Go ahead. Live out loud.

We talked about mindsets, energy awareness and making healthy choices. I promise you that your life will change when you make small shifts in each of these areas. When you get radical and make healthy decisions for you, your family wins too. Your job situations will shift. Everyone connected with you will be affected by the change in you. This is bigger than me. It is also bigger than you.

Radical ways to live boldly and courageously

- Live in full color
- Break out of your proverbial box
- Be spontaneous
- Go with the flow
- Do something outrageous
- Set fun goals
- Laugh often
- Say yes to what fully serves you
- Take more risks. At least you won't have to wonder what if….
- Give new opportunities and experiences a chance
- Expand your proverbial box or burn the box and be done with it

Today I celebrate.....

_____

_____

_____

Today I discovered....

_____

_____

_____

_____

I felt great when......

_____

_____

_____

_____

Your Path to Freedom and Bliss

Freedom means you are unobstructed in living your life as you choose. Anything else is a form of slavery.
Wayne Dyer

This has been an incredible experience. I am deeply honored to share it with you.

"You must learn a new way to think before you can master a new way to be." Marianne Williamson

I have in no way mastered this. I'm sure that when and if I do that there will be something else for me to learn. I am growing. I will continue to be on a growth cycle. I am committed to stay on this path to personal freedom. I want to see you there with me. I am here to serve you.

I believe in the freedom to choose. I am not concerned with how Webster defines love, freedom, abundance or bliss. I am more in tune with words that evoke the feeling of freedom for me. These words or phrases represent how I feel or felt when in a blissful state. Or words that represent how I am feeling now from this space of expansion. Connect with the special moments when you felt loved, free, or abundant. Get in touch with what that represents for you.

self-love days |sleeping in | spontaneous escapes| freedom to do what I want when I want and how I want it |adventure| fearless |sexy |finding my voice| feeling seen| ambiance| travel| unapologetic| spiritually connected | plush| luxurious| connection| acceptance| fine dining | clarity | magnificence | intuitive | sisterhood| beautiful | active | hiking| long walks| trapeze | soulful | huggable |lovable | kissable | organized| kinetic | expansive | authentic |community| being heard |empathetic| emotionally safe| sunset| training |sunrise | floating | belonging | wellness| ocean view | teaching | playful | healthy | orgasmic |radical | powerful | feminine | family time | romance | jovial |enthusiastic | spacious| glam squad | dream team |global |motherhood | speaking| pampered | radiant | courageous |cultural experiences| dance | breakthrough | aha moments |serving others | volunteer | endless opportunities | unstoppable | unshakable | unbreakable| unapologetic | friendship | generosity | gratitude | entertainment | discoveries| explorations | coaching | calm | fragrance | botanical gardens| owning my space| timeless | innovation | unlimited access | relationship| intimacy | quality time with people I love |laughter | warm fuzzy memories |debt free | spa days |flexibility| quality conversations| sophistication | relaxation | financial health |grandchildren | curiosity| new beginnings| love stories | falling in love |support | resourceful | creative expression| earthy | bohemian chic | bourgeois| fulfillment | wisdom |God-centered | lavish | storytelling | peak experiences| games| skipping | acknowledgment| juicy| spicy |sweet| grace and ease |effortless| free flowing| waterfalls| time freedom| freedom of choice | in great company | heart-centered | aligned values| legacy

You and I are here on assignment. We may experience similar lessons. We may even have some of the same teachers and mentors, but your timing and the way it unfolds is uniquely yours

Your path to freedom and bliss awaits you. I say "your path" not the path because my journey is not yours and yours is not your friend's and so on. You will experience abundance, joy and peace at the level in which you are open to receive it. Your destiny will align with your own personal awareness, mindset and choices.

You have an all access pass to love, freedom and bliss but only if you choose it. Will you? Will you seize your moment? Will you walk through the fire to reach your destiny in spite of fear, in spite of what others may say, in spite of not knowing all the details about how it will unfold?

My question to you is this. Are you willing to get radical in your love for yourself? Are you ready to become unapologetic, unbreakable and unstoppable? I believe that you are. It is time to claim your stake in the ground and make your presence known. You are free to put your big girl panties on and play full out. Rise up my sister! Rise up! Lean into the beauty of who God designed you to be. Your life is waiting for you.

Love and Blessings,

Melanie

Review

- Celebrate the beauty of you
- Mind your thoughts
- Live abundantly
- Get radical with your dreams.
- Relationship equity has powerful. Connections are key
- Remain aware of your energy
- Activate radical love for yourself
- Unimaginable love is available to you
- Peace is real and available to you
- Remain present and cherish every second of your life
- Accept support. Receiving help is not a disease. It is a gift and a blessing.
- The only person to compare yourself is who you used to be.
- Stand in unapologetic power.
- Feel. Process. Release. Keep it simple and keep it moving.
- Get radical! Create the life you want. Live boldly. Love courageously.
- Your path to freedom and bliss is available to you. Radical Love is real. Believe it. Receive it. Enjoy it. Share it with the world.

Our Thoughts Are Prayers
Words and Music by Lucille K. Olson

Our thoughts are prayers, and we are always praying.
Our thoughts are prayers; listen to what you're saying.
Seek a higher consciousness, a state of peacefulness,
And know that God is always there,
And every thought becomes a prayer.

Our thoughts are prayers, the tools that we create with.
Our thoughts are prayers that Spirit resonates with.
Seek a higher consciousness, a state of mindfulness,
And know that God is always there,
And every thought becomes a prayer.

Radical Gratitude

Wow! We made it through. My heart is overflowing with gratitude. This may be the longest acknowledgment ever.

First, I want to thank Mother for teaching me the power of pen and paper. I also thank you for giving me space to find my voice.

To my hubby, Sean, thank you for continuing to stand with me through mood swings and for checking in with me during my all-nighters. Thanks for the spontaneous hotel escapes to shift the environment for me to access my creative flow. Most importantly, thank you for opening your heart to me to experience unimaginable love. You said that you knew you loved me the day we met. You've stuck to that story for 15 years. Guess what? I finally believe you. ...wink wink

To my amazing daughter, Trinity, I have yet to find the adjective to accurately describe the love I have for you. You will forever be my heart's greatest treasure. Thank you for reminding me to stand in my brilliance as I watch you honor your own. Your strong truly is beautiful.

To my sons, know that I love and believe in you. Andrew, I really appreciated you checking in to ask "How's the book coming?"

Beverly and Elaine, I am grateful for your collaborative efforts throughout the editing process. You came through when I really needed you. How lucky am I to have you?!!

Karen, our bond is too special to articulate. I am grateful to you for allowing me to be me no matter what.

Bruce, thank you for the many thought-provoking conversations and for celebrating small wins with me.

My siblings, aunts, uncles, cousins, nieces and nephews, I cannot thank you enough for proving me wrong. My old belief was that people I love would reject me if I become achieved a certain level of success. You consistently stand with me throughout my failures and my successes.

Kashmere, you push me through by bridging the generational gap and keeping me connected to my silly side. I love you to pieces.

Miki, you really are my soul sister. I cannot thank you enough for the endless conversations full of laughter, storytelling and sometimes tears. I can always count on you to tell me the truth.

Special thanks to my phenomenal tribe of sisters, Bernada, Britt, Donna, Julie, Masika, Nikki and Tiffany. I am sending radical vibes in your direction. I am forever grateful to you for creating a safe space for me to process my thoughts, my fears and my celebrations. I am so blessed to have you.

To my clients and coaches, thank you for calling me forth and igniting the fire within me. You keep my vision alive.

Monica, I am so glad that you said 'Yes'. We bonded with grace and ease. I thank God for this divine connection.

Nikelle, thank you for your creative flow. You captured the essence of Freedom and Bliss on the 1st draft. How awesome are you?!!!

To Dad, Madear and Aunt Mae, I feel you smiling from above. I love and miss you dearly.
God, I am deeply honored that you gave me the words and trusted me to speak them responsibly. Thank you for holding me as I grew up and learned to deepen my love for myself.

A moment of Radical Self-Love:

Melanie, I am so proud of you for showing up in your own life. You gave yourself permission to be perfectly imperfect and vulnerable to the world. I celebrate you for trusting your inner wisdom on this project. You acknowledged your inner critic and pressed forward anyway. I have never been more proud of you. I love you. Keep shining!

About the Author

Melanie is a wife, mother, daughter, sister, friend, advocate and love enthusiast who devotes her time to empowering professional women how to align their self-care with business goals. Melanie is on a mission to arm women -- and teen girls on the cusp of womanhood -- with the tools to reach their destination, unapologetically saying, 'Yes' to themselves, 'Yes' to their heart's desires and 'Yes' to living a bold and courageous life. She has been featured on Fox32 News, TEW Radio, EmPowered to Radio, and Rejoice 102.3 FM Radio. Melanie's gentle, yet no nonsense approach and expertise leads women to breakthroughs that position them for lifelong success.

In her free time Melanie enjoys date nights with her husband Sean, quiet evenings and quality time with family and friends. She embraces her corny side, laughing at her own jokes, walking and skipping.

Made in the USA
Middletown, DE
15 May 2016